Reality
and
Evangelical Theology

The 1981 Payton Lectures

Reality
and
Evangelical Theology

by
T. F. Torrance

The Westminster Press
Philadelphia

Copyright © 1982 T. F. Torrance

BOOK DESIGN BY ALICE DERR

First edition

Published by The Westminster Press®
Philadelphia, Pennsylvania

PRINTED IN THE UNITED STATES OF AMERICA
9 8 7 6 5 4 3 2 1

Library of Congress Cataloging in Publication Data

Torrance, Thomas Forsyth, 1913–
  Reality and evangelical theology.

  (The 1981 Payton lectures)
  Includes bibliographical references and index.
  1. Revelation. 2. Religion and science—
1946–   . 3. Truth (Christian theology)
I. Title. II. Series: Payton lectures ; 1981.
BT127.2.T67 1982   231.7′4   81-19811
ISBN 0-664-24401-7   AACR2

To
Hywel D. Lewis
Philosopher and Theologian
in deep appreciation and gratitude

Contents

Preface

This book comprises The Payton Lectures delivered in April 1981 at Fuller Theological Seminary, Pasadena, California, under the title *The Realist Basis of Evangelical Theology*. The aim of the lectures was to cut a swath through the prevailing confusion about the nature of theological and biblical interpretation of divine revelation, so that Christ clothed with his gospel may be allowed to occupy the controlling center of the church's life, thought, and mission in the world today. That is what evangelical theology in the proper sense is about, in its ontological commitment to the incarnate presence and activity of God in Jesus Christ within the objectivities and intelligibilities of our human existence in space and time. Evangelical theology serves both the reality of God's articulate self-revelation to mankind and the reality of the creaturely world to which we belong, in the integrity and wholeness of the life, teaching, and activity of the historical and risen Jesus Christ.

I have tried to show in a number of previous works that understanding of Christ and the gospel becomes confused whenever it gets trapped within a cultural framework of thought in which our knowing and what we know are split apart and our inquiries are cut loose from an underlying and coherent substructure in our apprehension of reality. We find the same kind of confusion arising within science or philosophy when, owing to some kind of epistemological dichotomy, the logico-linguistic forms of thought with which we work are torn apart from and are only artificially related to the material content of knowledge. In this event extreme positions regularly arise and conflict with one another, positions such as a rationalist conventionalism and a materialist instrumentalism in science, or a pragmatic existentialism and a logical positivism in philosophy. Corresponding to these contrapositions there constantly arise in theology rationalist and empiricist extremes such as the docetism and ebionitism that emerged as soon as the Christian message was interpreted within the dualist structures of Hellenic culture, or the fundamentalism and liberalism that have for so long afflicted modern theology, not to mention the host of pseudo problems and contrived solutions that constantly attend these extremes. What ultimately gives rise to such a state of affairs is a damaging breach in the ontological bearing of our minds upon reality and its intrinsic intelligibility in the field of inquiry, in science, theology, or philosophy. Evidently it is by repairing the ontological relation of the mind to reality, so that a structural kinship arises between human knowing and what is known, that we may recover the natural integration between empirical and theoretical factors in our knowledge and thereby dissipate the confusion that comes from their disjunction. At the same time this should have the effect of restoring a unifying order into the foundations of all human knowing within the universe which God has made, and made to be one, and which he means us to explore and progressively to bring to faithful expression in appropriate sciences.

Now since God has endowed his creation with a rationality and beauty of its own in created correspondence to his transcendent rationality and beauty, the more the created universe unfolds its marvelous symmetries and harmonies to our scientific inquiries, the more it is bound to fulfill its role as a theater which reflects the glory of the Creator and resounds to his praise. But this is the very universe to which we human beings belong and which God has ordained as the creaturely medium through which he makes himself known to mankind, in his historical dialogue with Israel and above all in the incarnation of his Word in Jesus Christ; therefore the increasing scientific understanding of the universe, as under God it becomes disclosed to our inquiries, must be taken into account in our continuing appropriation of divine revelation and our deepening understanding of his self-communication in Jesus Christ. That is to say, in proportion to the seriousness with which we acknowledge the reality of God's self-revelation within the realities of the created order of space and time, we will be open to all that is new in the disclosure of the God-given rationality of the contingent universe. Far from detracting from faithful reception of God's articulate self-revelation in Israel and in Jesus Christ, or therefore from the primacy of the Old and New Testament Scriptures which continue to mediate that divine revelation, genuine scientific discovery of the world that God has made and unceasingly sustains by the creative power of his Word can only serve to draw us nearer to God in accordance with the way he has actually taken in making himself known to us within the objectivities and intelligibilities of our spatiotemporal existence. Our evangelical commitment to Jesus Christ "through whom and for whom the whole universe has been created," as Paul expressed it, will not allow us to divorce redemption from creation, but compels us to give the empirical reality of the created order its full and proper place in theological interpretation of divine revelation, especially in its incarnate form and reality in Jesus Christ. That is the inescapable *realism* of evangelical theology.

There is little doubt that the astonishing advance of physical science in its discovery of objective truth about the universe has much to teach theological science about realism, as through the sheer rigor of its research and the disciplined fidelity of its knowing to the nature of things it has been forced to replace a positivist and conventionalist understanding by a realist understanding of natural law. The more we know of the universe today, the more we find that we have to do with states of affairs governed by an inherent rationality independent of our scientific observations and theories, a rationality which is always and everywhere utterly reliable and which, while commanding our respect and rational assent, retains a mysterious transcendence over all our understanding and knowledge of it. Thus while our science is pursued in passionate commitment to the objective reality of the universe and under the compelling claims of its intrinsic rationality upon our minds and is dedicated to the task of making contact with reality and grasping it in the depth of that rationality, this does not mean that we are ever able by our science to capture that reality within our conceptual structures and theoretical formalizations. The very reality we grasp is possessed of a rationality of such an indefinite range that it outstrips all that we can think or say, conceive or formulate, about it. Precisely in disclosing itself to us in its independent reality and lending itself to our objective knowledge of it, the universe confers relativity on all our knowledge of it. Scientific theories and formalizations of law have their objectivity and truth in referring to real states of affairs beyond themselves and are therefore always revisable in the light of further disclosure from those real states of affairs. That is to say, the reality of the universe retains its own authority over all our inquiry and understanding, and remains the final judge of the truth or falsity of our concepts and statements about it. This is the kind of realism in which objectivity and relativity, properly understood, belong inseparably together.

How much more should a realism of this kind characterize theological inquiry and doctrinal formulation! Here we
have to reckon above all with the unique Reality and transcendent Rationality of the Lord God who created the universe out of nothing and gave it a contingent reality in utter
differentiation from his own and a contingent rationality in
continuous dependence on his own. By its very nature the
self-revelation of this God summons us to acknowledge the
absolute priority of God's Word over all the media of its
communication and reception, and over all understanding
and interpretation of its Truth. The Word and Truth of God
reach us and address us on their own free ground and on
their own authority, for they cannot be understood, interpreted, far less assessed for what they are, on any other
ground except that which they constitute, or by any other
standard besides themselves. Hence in all our response to
God's Word and in all formulation of divine Truth we are
summoned to let God retain his own reality, majesty, and
authority over against us. In divine revelation we have to do
with a Word of God which is what it is as Word of God in
its own reality independent of our recognition of it, and we
have to do with a Truth of God which is what it is as Truth
of God before we come to know it to be true. That means
that in all our response to God's self-revelation as it is mediated to us in space and time through the Holy Scriptures
we must seek to understand and interpret it in accordance
with its intrinsic requirements and under the constraint of
the truth which bears upon our minds in and through it, and
not in accordance with requirements of thought which we
bring to it or under the constraint of rigid habits of belief
which we retain at the back of our minds irrespective of
what we may experience beyond ourselves. Divine revelation which commands a response of this kind is very disturbing, for it uproots us from the comfortable certainty of our
preconceptions and calls in question the mechanisms we

constantly develop in order to give a firmness to our evangelical beliefs in themselves as beliefs, rather than in the
objective ground to which as beliefs they are properly correlated and in reference to which they are always open to
revision.

The ultimate fact with which we have to come to terms
in all theological and biblical interpretation—one which
Karl Barth has hammered home throughout all his immense
work—is that while God is who he is in his self-revelation,
that divine revelation is God himself, for it is not just something of himself that God reveals to us but his very own Self,
his own ultimate Being as God. Twice over, Barth used to
point out, the church in history has had to contend in a
major way for this evangelical conviction. Throughout the
fourth century the ancient church found itself compelled, in
fidelity to the gospel mediated through the apostolic revelation, to acknowledge in formal credal statement that what
God is toward us in Jesus Christ and in the Holy Spirit he
is in himself in his own eternal Being as God. That is to say,
any disjunction between God and his self-revelation
through Christ and in the Spirit could only mean that in the
last analysis the gospel is empty of any divine reality or
validity. What God reveals of himself and what he is in
himself are one and the same—hence the insistence by patristic theology that Jesus Christ the incarnate Son and the
Holy Spirit are each of one and the same being with God
the Father. That is the epistemological as well as the soteriological significance of the *homoousion.*

The same conviction was once more at stake in the sixteenth century when the struggle centered on the doctrine
of the free unconditioned grace of God, and it became clear
that grace is to be understood as the impartation not just of
something from God but of God himself. In Jesus Christ and
in the Holy Spirit God freely gives himself to us in such a
way that the Gift and the Giver are one and the same in the

wholeness and indivisibility of his Grace, and as such must be continually given and received. If in the fourth century the Christian church clarified the fact that, in making himself accessible to us in the incarnation once and for all through the Son and in the Spirit, God himself is the real content of his revelation, the church in the sixteenth century clarified the fact that, in his continuous self-revealing and self-giving through the Son and in the Spirit, God himself remains the real content of his revelation, for what he freely reveals of himself and his actual self-revealing are one and the same. If patristic theology found it had to stress the presence of the Being of God in the act of his revelation, Reformation theology found it had to stress the immediate act of God in the presence of his Being as revealed. Quite evidently—and this is the point of Barth's theology—both these are complementary, the Being of God in his Act and the Act of God in his Being, as he is eternally in himself as God and as he is toward us through Christ and in the Spirit. Thus in fidelity to the essence of the gospel it is the trinitarian understanding of God as he is in himself and as he is in his saving activity on our behalf that is found to uphold and control an evangelical understanding of divine revelation.

It would seem that these basic issues are once more at stake. Modern liberal theology like ancient Arianism continues to stumble at the identity between God and his revelation, which is evident not only in its denial of the deity of Jesus Christ but in its assimilation of the Spirit of Jesus Christ to the human spirit. Thus in rejecting a controlling center of God's self-revelation which is grounded both in the Reality of God and in the realities of our world, liberal theology is thrown back upon the autonomous religious reason to provide the ground on which all that is claimed to be divine revelation is to be considered, and therefore also the standards by which it is to be judged. Thus in the last analysis it is not, as in rigorous science or theology, reality itself that

is the ultimate judge of the truth or falsity of our thought
and speech about it, but the self-conscious and self-referring
human spirit. The ontological breach between Jesus Christ
and God is complemented by an ontological breach between the human mind and reality, but it is probably the
axiomatic acceptance of the latter breach which leads to the
former. An unquestioned epistemological, not to speak of
a cosmological, dualism results in the detachment of Christ
from God and then inevitably in the detachment of Christi-
anity from Christ and its steady disintegration within the
patterns of a pluralist society and its fragmented culture.

Our interest in this book, however, is also, and not least,
with the other extreme in the church of today, an evangelical fundamentalism which is passionately dedicated to preserve the integrity of the biblical faith. Fundamentalism
stumbles, not so much at the consubstantial relation between Jesus Christ and God the Father, at least so far as his
person is concerned, but at the consubstantial relation between the free continuous act of God's self-communication
and the living content of what he communicates, especially
when this is applied to divine revelation in and through the
Holy Scriptures. It rejects the fact that revelation must be
continually given and received in a living relation with God
—i.e., it substitutes a static for a dynamic view of revelation.
Here also a basic dualism is at work, not unlike that of
Newtonian science, which operated with a rigid homogeneous framework of ideas which it clamped down upon
phenomena without allowing the framework to be modified
by the ongoing experience of reality, even though the ideas
it comprised were themselves originally derived by way of
idealization from empirical experience in space and time.
This was necessary, it was claimed, in order to give a deter-
minate scientific account of the behavior of bodies in motion. Likewise fundamentalism operates with a rigid framework of beliefs which have a transcendent origin and which

are certainly appropriated through encounter with God in
his self-revelation and as such have an objective pole of
reference and control, but these beliefs are not applied in
a manner consistent with their dynamic origin and nature.
Instead of being open to the objective pole of their reference in the continual self-giving of God and therefore continually revisable under its control, they are given a finality
and rigidity in themselves as evangelical beliefs, and are
clamped down upon Christian experience and interpretation of divine revelation through the Holy Scriptures. Thus
they are endowed with a fixity at the back of the fundamentalist mind, where they are evidently secure from critical
questioning, not only on the part of skeptical liberals and
other freethinkers, but on the part of a divine self-revealing
which is identical in its content with the very Being of God
himself. At this point the epistemological dualism underlying fundamentalism cuts off the revelation of God in the
Bible from God himself and his continuous self-giving
through Christ and in the Spirit, so that the Bible is treated
as a self-contained corpus of divine truths in propositional
form endowed with an infallibility of statement which provides the justification felt to be needed for the rigid framework of belief within which fundamentalism barricades itself.

The practical and the epistemological effect of a fundamentalism of this kind is to give an infallible Bible and a set
of rigid evangelical beliefs primacy over God's self-revelation which is mediated to us through the Bible. This effect
is only reinforced by the regular fundamentalist identification of biblical statements about the truth with the truth
itself to which they refer. Here undoubtedly we find a
marked failure to acknowledge the unique Reality of God
in its transcendent authority and majesty over all the contingent media employed by God in his self-revelation to mankind. But what must be particularly distressing for a genu-

inely evangelical approach is that the living reality of God's self-revelation through Jesus Christ and in the Spirit is in point of fact made secondary to the Scriptures. Regarded from this point of view, fundamentalism appears to stumble also at the full consubstantiality of the incarnate Son and Word with God the Father, for it is evidently unwilling to acknowledge the identity in being between what God is toward us in his revelation in Jesus Christ and what he is in his living Being and Reality in himself. This would mean that the decisive problem of fundamentalism is not so different after all from the problem of liberalism. Both appear to balk at the fact that God himself is the one ultimate Judge of the truth or falsity, the adequacy or inadequacy, of all human conceptions and statements about him. Even the Holy Scriptures must submit to his judgment and thus point us away from themselves to the truth as it is in Jesus Christ.

This problem takes on a sharper form in relation to the doctrine of free grace and the identification it implies between what God gives us in Jesus Christ for our salvation and God himself the Giver. With the Reformation, clarification of the issues involved centered on the doctrine of justification through Christ alone. The fact that, through the free grace of God, Jesus Christ is made our Righteousness means that we have no righteousness of our own. To be put freely in the right with God means that we and all our vaunted right are utterly called in question before God. Epistemologically, this means that to be put in the truth with God reveals that in ourselves we are in the wrong. Or, as Paul bluntly expressed it, "Let God be true and every man a liar." No one may boast of his own orthodoxy any more than he may boast of his own righteousness. Justification thus turns out to be the strongest statement of the objectivity of faith and knowledge. That is to say, the very beliefs which we profess and formulate as obediently and carefully as we can in fidelity to God's self-revelation in Jesus Christ are themselves called into question by that revelation, for they have their truth not in themselves but in him to whom they refer, and are therefore constantly to be revised in the light of the Truth that Jesus Christ is in himself in God.

This is the crux at which fundamentalism is put to its severest test, when it should become clear whether it is genuinely evangelical or not, that is, ultimately obedient to Christ and his gospel or not. Does fundamentalism hold and apply its professed evangelical beliefs in a manner consistent with their origin in God's self-revelation in the incarnate life and work of Jesus Christ, and therefore in such a way that they point away from themselves to Jesus Christ alone as their truth and thereby acknowledge their own inadequacy and deficiency before him? This is a test before which fundamentalists frequently quail, for they appear to be trapped in a mental and theological inertia before the pain of justification by the grace of divine Reality alone, which threatens to wrench their minds free from inbuilt fixities and rigidities, so that they may be opened through the Spirit to the ultimate and creative Word and Truth of God himself. Radical change at this point would surely involve acknowledgment of the transcendent Reality and Authority of the living Jesus Christ not only over the church and all its doctrinal formulations but over the Holy Scriptures themselves. This would involve a discovery that the Scriptures have an authority and a compelling truth of a quite unfathomable kind, for they are grounded and anchored in the identity of God and his self-revelation to mankind through Christ and in the one Spirit.

I have tried to spell out at this point a little of what I mean by evangelical theology and its realist basis so that the reader may have some preliminary guide to the position which I advocate in the chapters that follow. I should like to thank the professors and students at Fuller Theological Seminary for their kindly reception of these lectures and the

serious attention they gave to the points raised. It was a
great privilege to lecture at a seminary that is so dedicated
to Jesus Christ and his gospel and to the interpretation of the
Bible. I do not forget the marvelous help the Seminary gave
me in preparing the typescript for publication, or the hospi-
tality generously accorded to me by staff and students alike.
My son the Rev. Dr. Iain R. Torrance, of Hillswick, Shet-
land, has very kindly helped me in reading the proofs and
preparing the indexes. I am very grateful for his constant
support and encouragement.

T.F.T.

Sea Spray, Canty Bay
East Lothian, Scotland

1.
The Bounds
of Christian Theology

It is distinctive of Christian theology that it treats of God in his relation to the world and of God in his relation to himself, not of one without the other. If it did not include the former, we who belong to the world could have no part in it, and if it did not include the latter, it could be concerned only with a "knowledge of God" dragged down and trapped within the world and our relations with it. Knowledge of God by *us* in our creaturely status within the world must indeed be knowledge of God in his interaction with us and the world he has made, but if it is to be knowledge of *God,* it must be grounded ultimately in the reality of God, in the inviolable otherness and intelligibility of God as he is in himself beyond our world altogether.

That was the point which John Duns Scotus had in mind when he formulated his famous distinction between *theologia in se* and *theologia in nobis,* or *theologia nostra.* [1] He recognized that authentic knowledge of God must be in accordance with the nature and mode of his divine being and must therefore involve a *real* and *actual* relation to God as its proper object, but he also held that we cannot have a knowledge of God cut off from the conditions of our present life in this world. He met this difficulty by distinguishing between different levels of knowledge which are related to

one another translogically, as it were, by his active condescension and self-manifestation to us in the world in such a
way that what God is in his relation to us he is in himself,
and what he is in himself he is in his relation to us in all
levels of our contingent existence and rationality.[2] Thus for
theological knowledge at all levels God remains its one
controlling and ultimate object. The supreme all-significant
level of knowledge is that which God has of himself in the
perfection of his own eternal Being, which Duns Scotus
calls *theologia in se*—the pure science of theology as it is in
God. It is from this divine ground in God that all knowledge of him by his creatures derives, and upon it all levels
of knowledge of God ultimately depend. *Theologia nostra*,
on the other hand, refers to such knowledge of God as is
mediated to us within the bounds and conditions of our life
in this world. Restricted and circumscribed as it is, and
refracted as it is through the damaging effect of sin upon our
relation with God, it is nevertheless grounded in God himself, who infinitely transcends what we can conceive of him
within the limits of our creaturely minds. If our theology
were not interpenetrated at least in some real measure by
God's knowledge of himself, it could not be real knowledge
of God; but nor could it be genuinely our theology if it were
not concerned with knowledge granted to us within the
bounds of our finite order of existence and thought.

A similar distinction had been drawn much earlier in
Greek patristic theology between knowledge of God which
he gives us through his "economic condescension" to us
within the objectivities and intelligibilities of the created
world of space and time, and knowledge of God as he is
eternally in himself in his own internal relations. Each is
coordinated with the other through the incarnation or the
"human economy" which the Son of God has undertaken
for our sakes—i.e., the ordered process of God's revealing
and redeeming activity in space and time, in which he has

both extrapolated, as it were, his divine mystery within the conditions of our human nature and at the same time lifted up our human nature into union and communion with himself.[3] Through the incarnation of his Son or Word, and in the Holy Spirit mediated through him, God the Father does not remain closed to us but has opened himself to our human knowing. Through Christ Jesus—as Paul expressed it—and in one Spirit we have access to the Father (Eph. 2:18). This meant that Christian theology had to advance beyond the traditional stress of Judaism upon the unknowability, namelessness, and undifferentiated oneness of God. In a struggle with the Platonic conception of God as "beyond all being and knowing" it was forced to unfold the trinitarian implications of the fact that God really makes himself accessible to us in his internal relations as Father, Son, and Holy Spirit.[4]

Everything hinges on the reality of God's *self*-communication to us in Jesus Christ, in whom there has become incarnate, not some created intermediary between God and the world, but the very Word who eternally inheres in the Being of God and is God, so that for us to know God in Jesus Christ is really to know him as he is in himself.[5] It is with the same force that attention is directed upon the Holy Spirit, whom the Father sends through the Son to dwell with us, and who, like the Son, is no mere cosmic power intermediate between God and the world, but is the Spirit of God who eternally dwells in him and in whom God knows himself, so that for us to know God in his Spirit is to know him in the hidden depths of his divine Being. Father, Son, and Holy Spirit are not just the operational modes which God's manifestations take in his saving contact with us in the transient conditions of our creaturely existence, and which could only have a metaphorical and not a real significance; they are distinct personal subsistences and relations of being which God is in his own eternal Reality as God, indepen-

dently of his revelation to us or of our knowing of him. That
is to say, the economic forms of God's self-communication
to us in history derive from and repose upon a communion
of Persons immanent in the Godhead. It is as our knowing
of God passes from what is called the "economic Trinity"
to the "ontological Trinity" that we have *theologia* in the
supreme and proper sense, knowledge of God on the free
ground of his own Being, knowledge of him in which our
knowing is controlled and shaped by relations eternally
immanent in God. Without this advance from knowledge of
God in his relations toward us *(quoad nos)* to at least some
measure of knowledge of God in himself *(quoad se)*, knowledge of God toward us is not ontologically grounded in
God, but is at the mercy of our knowledge of ourselves. If
God is not inherently and eternally in himself what he is
toward us in Jesus Christ, as Father, Son, and Holy Spirit,
then we do not really or finally know God at all as he is in
his abiding Reality.

From the perspective of its transcendental relation to
God, Christian theology must be considered as unbounded,
precisely because it treats of God who in his unlimited and
eternal Reality infinitely transcends our conceptions of him.
However, since we may know God only insofar as he has
condescended to accommodate his self-revelation to our
creaturely reality and the finite measures of our minds,
which are what they are through his design, Christian theology must be considered to be bounded by the actual way in
which God has chosen to relate himself to us in this world.
The only knowledge possible for us is that which he mediates to us in and through this world. We do not and cannot
know God in disjunction from his relation to this world, as
if the world were not his creation or the sphere of his
activity toward us. This is not to say that we reach knowledge of God by way of logical inference from the world, but
rather that we may know him only within the field of rela-

tions actually set up by God in his interaction with the world he has made, even though in that field we know him as the Creator of the universe who transcends it altogether. We know God, then, in such a way that our knowledge *(theologia nostra)* is correlated with the world as his creation and the appointed medium of his self-revelation and self-communication to mankind. Everything would go wrong if the creaturely reality of this world were confused with or mistaken for the uncreated Reality of God, or if knowledge of God were cut off from the fact that it is *our* knowledge, that is, knowledge of God by us in this world.

Before we proceed further, let us pause to reflect on this complex of relations: God/ourselves/world, or God/man/world, which appears to define for us the bounds of theology. Theology cannot be narrowed down to the relations of God and man alone. It is with God in his relation to the world that we are concerned, and with man in his relation to the world, that is, with the relation of this God to this man. That is why we cannot speak of God except within the world in which he has placed us, and of which man is by divine creation a primary constituent element. Theologically speaking, man and the universe belong together and together constitute what we mean by "world," the world in its relation to God. Man is an essential member of the creation, with a specific function to fulfill within it, as the *priest of nature* or the *priest of creation.* [6] Through his activity as a rational, articulating agent under God, the inherent intelligibility of the universe, in its stratified structures and multivariable order and harmony, comes to expression and articulation. That is what we find taking place in the natural sciences, and that is surely how sciences, at least from a theological point of view, are to be understood in relation to the universe which God has designed and which he continues to sustain in its being and order through his creative presence and power. Just as God made organic forms of life to reproduce themselves, so he has made the universe to develop and express itself as the creation of God. That is how the created universe is affected by man, for man is that primary constituent within it through whom it is destined to know itself and unfold its intrinsic rationality and significance. Man is not to be regarded as a stranger in the cosmos, and his scientific activity is not, or should not be, an imposition *ab extra* upon nature, for, properly regarded, it is a natural and intrinsic process in the continuous expansion of the universe from its divinely given initial conditions. It is when man for some reason is out of gear with nature, when he seeks to dominate it and make it serve an alien end, that he develops those processes of thought which intensify his alienation from nature and lead him into the chaos of meaninglessness and ecological confusion. Properly regarded and deployed, science is not a torment-ing of nature but rather the way in which nature, pregnant with new forms of being, comes to be in travail and to give birth to structured realities out of itself. Man the scientist is nature's midwife, as it were. Actually he is rather more than that, for his own rational nature is so deeply coordinated to the intrinsic rationalities of nature that he becomes the in-strument under God through which the intelligible uni-verse discloses its hidden secrets and unfolds out of its chrys-alis, as it were, in orderly and beautiful patterns of being. In these processes there becomes revealed an intelligibility beyond man's artifice and control, something absolutely given and transcendent, to which as man he is and must be rationally open and obedient, for that is his nature as a rational agent. Man acts rationally only under the compul-sion of reality and its intrinsic order, but it is man's specific vocation to bring it to word, to articulate it in all its wonder and beauty, and thus to lead the creation in its praise and glorification of God the Creator. With this priestly function which man exercises for the creation, scientific inquiry becomes a deeply religious duty in man's relation to God.

So far as theological science is concerned, then, it is evident that we must operate with a *triadic relation,* God/man/world or God/world/man, for it is this world unfolding under man's scientific inquiries which constitutes the medium in which God makes himself known and in which man may express knowledge of him. This implies, of course, that there is a necessary and inescapable relation between theological concepts and physical concepts, or between spiritual and natural concepts; between positive theology and natural theology, or rather between theology and natural science; for this is what it means to take seriously knowledge of God in his relation to the world. But it also implies that we are not really engaged in theology in the proper sense, and are not scientifically engaged with theology, if we restrict it to the God/man or man/God relationship.

A theology that is restricted to the relation between man and God is deficient and primitive, for it has not advanced from *mythos* to *logos,* from thinking out of a center in the human subject to thinking out of a center in objective reality, from thinking projectively in pictures and images to thinking in terms of structured imageless relations. Let me explain.

In primitive thinking we are concerned with observations and phenomena, describe things as they appear to us, and interpret their significance in relation to our desires, fears, needs, and abilities. There predominates a subject/object relation in which we operate with vision or observation as providing the model for knowledge. The external world of events and realities is apprehended and invested with meaning as it affects us and occasions experiences within ourselves, and so we tend to interpret it symbolically, that is, in terms of symbols, myths, or images evoking and expressing inward responses. Symbolical thinking of this kind always tends to be dominant in periods or cultures which are governed by a dualist outlook in the foundations of knowledge. For a typical instance of this, one could point in ancient times to Augustinian thought with its radical dichotomy between the realm of sense experience and the realm of intelligible truths, or in more modern times to Kantian thought with its dichotomy between a realm of phenomenal events and a realm of noumenal ideas, or between things as they appear to us and unknowable things in themselves. Augustinian and Kantian thought in different ways gave rise to highly symbolic interpretations of Christian theology, especially where it bears upon the concrete realities of space and time.

In scientific activity symbolic thinking does not disappear but in many ways is actually accentuated—for example, in the constant elaboration of symbolic systems or languages as methodological instruments whereby we may extend the range of our thought beyond what we would be capable of without them. The significance of these symbolic systems, however, does not lie in the systems themselves; far less is it to be found in serving the self-expression of their inventors or users. It is to be found in their bearing upon what is not symbolic, just as the significance of mathematics is to be found not in the mathematical equations themselves but in their bearing upon nonmathematical reality.[7] Thus while symbolic thinking does not disappear, it is made to serve the primary concern of scientific inquiry to understand things strictly in accordance with their natures and to interpret them in accordance with their intrinsic relations and significance, and to assist rigorous theoretic penetration into the structured interrelations of things in themselves in their objective states. In this way scientific inquiry engages with object/object relations in which our subject/object relations are controlled from beyond themselves by reference to the ontological structures of the realities being investigated. Thus the movement from primitive thinking to scientific thinking is one in which we pass from knowing things *quoad nos* to knowing them *quoad se.*

Judging from the history of thought in ancient as in modern times, it would seem evident that so long as theology is restricted to the man/God relationship it can hardly escape from the projective thrust of man's own self-understanding, so that theology tends to contract into a form of anthropology in which meaning is expressed in the symbolic or mythological objectification of inward experience. This always becomes accentuated under the stress of phenomenalist and dualist theories of knowledge in which the relation between subject and object, or intelligible form and ontological reality, is seriously damaged, if not severed. In this event theology quickly reduces to being a mere second-order activity in which there results a further split between form and content, and between method and subject matter, so that theological concepts become twice removed from objective reality. Signs or symbols, whether they are poetic myths or logical structures, now come to represent the inner spiritual world of the religious subject and become the vehicles of his deep anxieties and fantasies.[8] This is just as evident in a highly formalistic theology which takes refuge in the logical or grammatical manipulation of verbal symbols in order to escape the disturbing and compelling claims of objective truth, as it is of an existentialist approach to Jesus Christ which detaches faith in him from all empirical correlates in space and time lest it should succumb to critical attack from an objectivist natural science. However, when Christian theology takes seriously the God/world/man or God/man/world relation, the knowing subject is forced outside of himself, as it were, into the open field of God's creative interaction with the world of space and time, and his subject/object relations fall under the controlling orientation of object/object relations in the created universe as it becomes disclosed through scientific inquiry. That is the universe of objective but contingent intelligibility within which God has set man and where man is destined for communion with himself. That is the universe in which God makes himself known to man, and it is only within its bounds that real knowledge of God may arise.

There are several aspects of this *triadic relation,* God/man/world or God/world/man, within which a realist theology must operate, that we may now consider more fully.

1. THERE IS A SIGNIFICANT AREA OF OVERLAP BE-TWEEN THEOLOGICAL SCIENCE AND NATURAL SCI-ENCE.

The field in which theology operates is that set up through the constant interaction of God's uncreated intelligibility with the created or contingent intelligibilities of our world, or, looked at from a different angle, the field set up through the interaction of the order of redemption with the order of creation. However we consider it, it seems clear that theological science and natural science operate within the same world, and within the same medium, the medium of space and time, which are the bearers of contingent order or intelligibility in which all created realities share.[9] Within that medium, natural science is concerned to explore the stratified structures of contingent existence, and theological science inquires of God their Creator who reveals himself through them. Each science—theological science and natural science—operates in accordance with the nature of the realities it is investigating and the field structures that characterize it, and in accordance with its own distinctive objective, so that while the two sciences inevitably overlap within the space-time of this world, they move in different directions, one to investigate creaturely relations out of themselves, apart from God, and the other to inquire of God who transcends all creaturely relations and makes himself known through his Word as the Lord of all space and time. In both theological science and natural science, man himself is at work as the inquirer, so that the knowledge and its formulation which each enshrines cannot be cut off from the fact that it is, respectively, *man's* knowledge of God or *man's* knowledge of nature. While man himself inevitably comes into the center of the picture in this way, it is essentially as servant and not as master, for in both sciences, although in different ways, he acts under the compelling claims of his "object," God or the created universe, and in neither science can he be true and faithful to his objective without responsible commitment to that which he serves. Neither theological science nor natural science, therefore, can be pursued in an impersonal way as if man himself had no part to play in scientific inquiry and formulation, but, far from implying that this leads to diminished objectivity, the opposite is actually the case, for it is only man acting personally as a rational agent who is capable of engaging in genuinely objective operations.[10]

So far as theology is concerned there are two aspects of this triadic relation that I would like to stress.

a. Natural theology has its proper place and status within the area of overlap between natural science and theological science, that is, within the overlapping of created and uncreated intelligibility where natural science presses its inquiries in one direction and theological science presses its inquiries in another direction. It is, I believe, in this way that we have now to rethink the traditional distinction between what is called "natural theology" and what is variously called "positive theology" or "revealed theology" and the bearing they have on one another.

Of course much depends on whether we start from dualist foundations in knowledge or not, that is, whether we operate with a disjunction between form and being, or structure and substance, and whether epistemological dualism of this kind is accompanied, as it almost invariably is, by some form of cosmological dualism in which God is not thought of as interacting with the universe of space and time but as inertially related to it or as deistically detached from it. It has always been in periods when epistemological and cosmological dualism have predominated that the demand for a natural theology has been urgent, in order to find a way of throwing a logical bridge between the world and God if only to give some kind of rational support for faith. But as modern analysis has made clear again and again, no such logical bridge is possible any more than it is possible to erect logical connections between form and being or structure and substance. The whole situation changes radically, however, when dualist modes of thinking are undermined or set aside and a realist unitary theory of knowledge takes over, as has happened in modern times especially as the implications of the Maxwellian and Einsteinian approaches to the universe and its intrinsic intelligible relations have been worked out, not only for physics but for basic ways of knowing in every sphere of human inquiry. Now that the whole structure of physical science, and with it the whole structure of the universe as we understand it, has altered, and disjunctive ways of thinking have given way to integrative modes of thought, the significance of the overlap between natural scientific inquiry and theological inquiry has considerably increased. How, then, are we to think of natural theology in this new state of affairs?

I find it helpful here to think of the way in which geometry and physics have come to be integrated in the profoundly unitary outlook upon the universe that followed Einstein's rejection of the dualist outlook built into classical physics and mechanics by Newton, whose science was shaped by the framework of absolute mathematical time and space on the one hand and of relative apparent time and space on the other hand.[11] Immensely successful as Newtonian science was in advancing knowledge of the universe of bodies in motion, it operated with an idealized geometry detached from experience and erected into an independent conceptual system, and then used this as a homogeneous framework within which all physical knowledge was pursued and organized. Newtonian science gave rise to a relentlessly mechanistic conception of the universe which drove a widening chasm between the natural sciences and the humanities. As also became increasingly apparent, science of this kind could not account for quite fundamental features of the universe, such as the properties of radiation or the behavior of light, which are found to have a pervasive and primary role in the dynamic structure of the universe in its microcosmic as well as its macrocosmic aspects. Einstein traced the basic problem to the artificial separation between geometry and experience. He insisted that geometry must be brought into the midst of physics, where it could no longer function as an antecedent system on its own, immune from modification by our knowledge of empirical reality, but would be in fact a natural science integrated with physical science as a four-dimensional geometry. Far from being swallowed up by physics, however, geometry would become the epistemological structure in the heart of physics, although considered in itself it would be incomplete without physics.

It is in a similar way, I believe, that we must now think of natural theology in rejecting its traditional independent status. The old approach regarded natural theology as supplying a "preamble to faith," an independent conceptual system antecedent to actual knowledge of God, but that is to separate form from content and method from subject matter and cannot but have the effect of distorting our knowledge of God by forcing it into inapposite or misleading forms of thought. As in any rigorous science, so here in theological science we must let all preconceived forms or frameworks of thought be called into question by those which arise on the ground of actual empirical knowledge of God. It is in relation to these forms of thought, which press themselves upon our minds when we seek to know God in accordance with his nature and the steps he takes in making himself known to us, that natural theology can fulfill its proper function, but only in a changed form in which it constitutes the epistemological intrastructure of our knowledge of God. As such it cannot stand on its own feet as an independent conceptual or logical structure detached from the material content of our actual knowledge of God, although it is certainly open to conceptual or logical analysis. Such analysis reveals, however, that natural theology of this kind is essentially incomplete in itself and is what it should be and functions as it ought only as it is completed beyond itself in positive theology. Such an integration of the formal and material, or the theoretical and empirical, factors in our knowledge of God is entirely consistent with the switch from a dualist to a unitary basis of knowledge which rigorous theological science and natural science both demand. It is also consistent with the recognition that, since God has irreversibly incarnated his self-revelation in Jesus Christ, the Word made flesh, there cannot be two ways to knowledge of God, one in Jesus Christ and another behind his back, but only one way, through Christ and in his Spirit. Moreover, all this is again consistent with the recognition that, since the Word of God by whom all things were made and continue to be upheld became incarnate within the contingent, rational structures of space and time, within which theological science and natural science alike pursue their inquiries, there must be a much closer connection between the concepts deployed by theological and by natural science than is often realized, even when we take into account the necessary change in meaning that theological concepts involve in accordance with the nature of their divine Object.

   b. Empirical correlates have an essential place in any theology that seeks to be faithful both to the creation and to the incarnation. The necessity for empirical correlation of theological concepts and statements with the empirical creation is evident from the necessity but not the sufficiency of natural theology (in its transformed sense), which we have just discussed. If we cannot cut off knowledge of God either from the world of which he is the Creator or from ourselves who are creatures of this world, then theological concepts and statements can have meaning for us only when they are coordinated with empirical reality, even though within that coordination their reference, along with that of the contingent world, reaches out indefinitely beyond themselves to God the Creator and the ultimate source of all truth and rationality within the universe. This is not to argue that every theological concept or statement must have a specific empirical correlate, but that theological concepts and statements have a proper place in a coherent system which at certain essential points is correlated with the empirical world.

The stratified structure of our scientific knowledge of the universe, as Einstein, Polanyi, and others have shown us,[12] usually comprises three levels of thought coordinated with one another: the primary or basic level, which is the level of our ordinary day-to-day experience and knowledge; the secondary or scientific level; and the tertiary or metascientific level. The concepts organized at the tertiary level are coordinated with those organized at the secondary level, not through a one-to-one relation between them, but as the level by which they are organized and defined is coordinated with the lower level, where it is left open to it and where the higher level constitutes its controlling meta-level. Similarly, the concepts organized and defined at the secondary level are coordinated with the concepts at the primary level, which arise directly out of our experience as we interact with the world around us. Thus the concepts at the highest level are coordinated with those at the empirical level through cross-level relations; but without being grounded in that way in our actual experience and knowledge they are ultimately no more than empty, meaningless forms of thought.

Theological science also develops a stratified structure which rises from our immediate experience, knowledge, and worship of God in Jesus Christ in the life of the church, through the "economic" trinitarian relations at the theological level to the higher, controlling level of "ontological" trinitarian relations, which we have already noted.[13] It is not difficult to show that in such a structure theological science operates in a way that is not essentially different (at least in its intellectual aspect) from the way in which, for example, the field structures of space and time are coordinated with those in ongoing empirical reality which we seek to bring to light and expression in our scientific investigation of the physical universe. That theological concepts and statements, at whatever level they are organized and defined, must be correlated with empirical concepts and statements grounded in our actual day-by-day knowledge of God is inescapably implied by the interaction of God with us in the universe of space and time which he has created and endowed with its rational order, and which he continues to sustain by his immanent presence and power. That is the universe to which by creation we belong, and it is within it alone that God makes himself known to us and summons us to obedient response in life and knowledge. Spatial and temporal, physical and historical coefficients are the *sine qua non* of any realist theological understanding and formulation.

This is especially apparent, of course, from the way in which we have to think out the incarnation of God's Word as determining the actual place in physical space and time where God has communicated himself to us, where God and man are appointed to meet, and where spatiotemporally conditioned knowledge of him in Jesus Christ arises. But it is also evident in our very knowledge of God in Jesus Christ that instead of being resolved into or being boxed up in spatial and temporal presence, the presence of God the Creator of all space and time infinitely transcends them in his creating and upholding power. The incarnation means that we cannot really know God without faithful conformity to his actual revelation of himself to us in space and time, and therefore lays it down that we may not seek to steal knowledge of God, as it were, by climbing up some other way, that is, by transcending space and time or leaping beyond the limited conditions of our place on earth and in history. At the same time, the incarnation also means that the very God who has graciously condescended to be one with us in Jesus Christ in space and time grants us communion with himself in his Spirit in such a way that without taking leave of our spatiotemporal existence or our human senses and reason we may really know him in his eternal divine Reality which infinitely transcends all space and time. That we cannot have the latter experience without the former is decisively reinforced by the ascension of Christ, which has the effect of sending us back to the historical Jesus in space and time as the one place where we may meet and know God the Father, that is, to the life, teaching, passion, and resurrection of Jesus Christ, which we may not bypass if we really are to know God even in his eternal inner-trinitarian relations as Father, Son, and Holy Spirit. If, then, we consider the gospel at its decisive point, in the resurrection of Jesus Christ from the grave, it must be insisted that we empty it of any real or final significance when we think or speak of the resurrection without an empirical correlate in space and time such as the empty tomb.

Since a realist theology of this kind involves empirical coefficients, we must reckon on the need for dual control in

the testing and establishment of theological concepts and
statements. We are familiar with dual control elsewhere—
for example, in engineering and in biological science. Both
in engineering and in biology we operate with operational
principles over and above the laws of physics and chemistry
which obtain at a lower level, but which are open to control
from beyond themselves at their boundary conditions.
These operational principles depend on the laws of physics
and chemistry at their lower levels and are to that extent
determined by them, and therefore our understanding and
formulation of them must be tested by reference to the laws
of physics and chemistry. However, engineering or organis-
mic operations are not explainable merely by reference to
the laws of physics and chemistry, for they embody at their
higher level connections of a different kind with quite new
factors which are not reducible to physico-chemical connections, and therefore require to be controlled and tested in
a different way in accordance with their distinctive nature
and operation. It is in a similar way, *mutatis mutandis,* that
we have to think out and test our understanding of the event
of the resurrection of Jesus Christ from the dead, for it is at
once an event within space and time and a creative act of
God within space and time. Quite clearly the empirical
correlates of the resurrection have to be appreciated and
controlled through reference to genuine spatiotemporal
coordinates and connections, but since the resurrection is
not an event that can be explained merely in terms of contingent connections in space and time, it must also be appreciated and controlled through reference to the saving act
of God in Jesus Christ and in its consistence with the whole
self-revelation of God to us in him. That is to say, we have
to think conjunctively at two levels at the same time, if we
are to understand the resurrection of Christ as an event that
embodies within spatiotemporal conditions, without abro-
gating them, a divine act which injects a new dimension into

the situation within which the spatiotemporal correlates are controlled at their boundary conditions and are made to serve the divine purpose of redemption and re-creation.

2.THEOLOGICAL SCIENCE OPERATES WITH AN INSEPARABLE RELATION BETWEEN THE EMPIRICAL AND THE THEORETICAL.[14]

What is meant here by the "empirical" is not just what is sensible and tangible so much as the *experienced imperceptible and intangible.* For an analogy taken from natural science which may be helpful, reference may be made to the space-time structure of the metrical field, which is inherently invisible or unobservable but which is nevertheless regulative of all our creaturely and phenomenal experience.

The inseparability of the empirical and the theoretical is of particular importance wherever we are concerned with the relation of theological concepts and statements to empirical correlates in the sense which we have just been discussing. Where is this of more pressing importance than in the place that history and the handling of historical events and historical evidence have in Christian theology, not least with respect to the historical Jesus Christ and the historico-critical approach required in our understanding and interpretation of the presentation of Jesus Christ embedded in the Gospels handed down to us? The problem has been seriously complicated by the predominant stress on phenomenalism and observationalism in post-Newtonian science, and especially in the post-Kantian era, when a huge gap opened up between the phenomenal and the noumenal, or things as they appear to our human observation and things as they are alleged to be in themselves. Here we have a systematization of the notion that there is nothing in the mind but what is first in the senses, and a restriction of scientific knowledge to what can be demonstrated from observation or can be deduced from observational data through logical operations. This implied that the concepts and relations of ideas with which scientific inquiry and formulation must operate do not derive from an intelligibility inherent in empirical reality, independent of our knowing of it, but from the built-in structures of our intuition and understanding. In the last resort, therefore, scientific theories have to be regarded not as having a descriptive reference to structures in being but as convenient or operationally effective arrangements of our observational data. That is to say, on this view of scientific knowledge there is no intrinsic but only a conventional relation between the empirical and the theoretical.

Modern realist science, however, has been forced to take a very different view of the relation between the empirical and the theoretical ingredients in knowledge, for they are grounded upon the inherence of empirical and theoretical factors in one another in reality itself. It is this objective interconnection between the empirical and the theoretical, or the observational and the conceptual, which has proved to be of such far-reaching significance in the great shift that has taken place in our understanding of the physical universe and indeed of the structure of physical science. In discussing the distorting effect of a split between the observational and the conceptual ingredients in scientific inquiry, F. S. C. Northrop has illuminatingly pointed to the difficulties a social scientist created for himself in his study of the Navajo Indians in the southwest section of the United States.[15] After many years of observation he came to realize that for all his direct observations he had failed to understand them. He had taken great care to ensure that the sensed data he collected were as objective as possible, but the concepts he used to describe, integrate, and interpret his objectively sensed impressions were not really those of the Navajo Indians. He came to realize that a really objective knowledge of the Navajo people and their culture required him, as a scientific investigator, to interpret what he observed by the concepts used by the Navajos themselves in the development of their culture, rather than by concepts he was already familiar with from his own white man's culture or his own school of social science. His failure to understand the Navajos properly and even to observe them properly had its basis in an alien way of conceptualizing the cultural phenomena he had been studying. That is to say, the conceptual ingredient for controlled empirical observation must be one naturally intrinsic to the field being investigated. There are no so-called bare observational facts, but only facts that are already laden with meaning, which have to be observed and interpreted out of their latent intelligibility.

Michael Polanyi has pointed again and again in the same direction, among other ways, by showing what happens when we use inverting spectacles which disrupt the coincidence of visual and mental images in our orientation to the world around us.[16] When we put on spectacles of this kind, severe disorientation results and it takes usually about eight days of adjustment. During this process it is not the perceptual image that changes, for it remains constant, but a new conceptual image needs to be integrated with it if we are once again to regain the kind of orientation to the world about us which we need if we are to behave rationally in accordance with the objects and obstacles we encounter. Rational behavior involves the inhering of perceptual and conceptual images in one another, and irrational behavior results when they are split apart.

What may we learn, then, from this integration of the empirical and the theoretical components in knowledge for a realist Christian theology? The answer must surely be that we may learn the importance of a genuinely *theological* approach to our source material, which nevertheless does not discount the empirical correlates which we have discussed —that is, an approach in which we refuse to countenance a

split between ontological and intelligible ingredients in
what we seek to know, or a split between empirical and
theoretical components in our knowledge of it and subsequent articulation of that knowledge. So far as the biblical
texts are concerned, this calls for an unashamed theological
exegesis and interpretation of them, if only to control our
historico-grammatical and historico-critical research so that
it may be properly objective. So far as the interaction of God
with mankind in his revealing and saving activity through
Israel and in Jesus Christ is concerned, to which the biblical
texts bear witness, this calls for a movement of thought in
which we seek to penetrate beyond the subject/object relations (which is the level of phenomenalist observation) into
the intelligible interrelations of the realities signified and
attested by the Holy Scriptures which are nevertheless independent of the Scriptures. Thus theological exegesis and
interpretation of the Holy Scriptures would go along with
and be controlled by theological understanding of the divine truths and realities they mediate to us, but theological
understanding of those truths and realities would themselves be controlled by constant theological exegesis and
interpretation of the biblical texts. Through a theological
approach of this kind, a realist evangelical theology will go
far toward healing the artificial gap that has opened up in
modern times between kerygma and dogma, exegesis and
dogmatics, and thereby toward restoring to Christian theology rigorous fidelity to its proper subject matter, the self-
communication and self-revelation of God in Jesus Christ
his incarnate Word.

3. THEOLOGICAL SCIENCE IS CONCERNED WITH THE
DISTINCTIVE KIND OF ORDER THAT OBTAINS IN ONTO-
RELATIONS.

Generally speaking, what is meant by "onto-relation" is
the kind of relation subsisting between things which is an

essential constituent of their being, and without which they would not be what they are. It is a being-constituting relation. Something like this has recently emerged in particle theory, which has had to move away from the analytical concept of separated particles with which classical science operated. Particles are found to interpenetrate and contain one another in such a way that the relations between particles are just as ontologically significant as the particles themselves. In the history of thought a primary instance of an onto-relational reality is the *person,* for relations between persons enter into their being as persons. The concept of "person," however, is a direct product of Christian theology, and specifically of the doctrines of Christ and the Holy Trinity. Once the concept of person, hitherto unknown in antiquity, was launched into the developing stream of human thought, it inevitably acquired a history of its own, which has constantly tended to obscure its theological import. The difficulty may be indicated by contrasting the definitions of person offered by Boethius and Richard of St.-Victor. The Boethian definition of person is a philosophical concept derived through logical analysis from Aristotelian and Neoplatonic notions of particular and general substance and rational nature.[17] The Ricardine definition, however, is a theological concept reached by way of ontological derivation from the communion of Love in the Being of God between Father, Son, and Holy Spirit, who wholly interpenetrate and coinhere in one another in such a way that their personal distinctness as Father, Son, and Holy Spirit remains inviolate.[18] The Triune God is not only a fullness of personal Being in himself, but is also person-constituting Being. It was from theological understanding of God's personal and personalizing self-communication, creating personal reciprocity between us and himself, that the Christian concept of the person arose, which is applicable in a creaturely way to persons in relation to one another but which reflects the transcendent way in which the three divine Persons are interrelated in the Holy Trinity.

Our immediate concern here, however, is not with the onto-relational concept of person but with the distinctive kind of *order* that inheres in onto-relations of this kind. It is essentially a dynamic ontological structure (perhaps akin to field structure in relativistic physics) in which form, motion, and being are inextricably intertwined. By its nature it is not the kind of order that can be grasped and expressed through abstracting its form, for that would disembody and destroy it, or through analytical breakdown of its dynamic structure, for that would transpose it into something quite different. It is not subject therefore to logical determination or formalization, for it must be apprehended in its own intelligible wholeness and its own interior power of organization. It may be cognized through nonanalytical, empirico-theoretical penetration into its dynamic structure guided by basic clues which we intuitively apprehend as we allow our minds to fall under the power of its distinctive intelligibility.

By way of an analogy from the world of natural science, which is admittedly not altogether apt, let me point to work that has been done in recent years on crystals. Crystalline formations embody a polycentric form of order which does not yield to physico-chemical analysis or logical construction. While we cannot get very far in explaining this kind of order through analytical methods, we are able to create certain conditions within which crystalline formations spontaneously become disposed into a distinctive order. In this event useful recourse is made to group theory in developing appropriate modes of apprehension in the light of intuitively apprehended clues which press themselves upon us as we work with crystals. One can point to a similar state of affairs in biology, in the multivariable kind of morphological order which we find in organic life, which has been calling forth the development of system theory to cope with it in an intelligibly appropriate way. In both of these instances we have to abandon the notion that the rational is accessible to logico-analytical processes in the conviction that here we have to do with intelligible order of a kind that is too interiorly rich and unitary for that rather simplistic and reductionist approach. It may be apprehended and interpreted only through distinctive modes of rational thought on our part appropriate to its nature. This means that we have a lot of hard new work to do in developing the appropriate conceptual instrumentality through which to allow our minds to fall under the power of this kind of order, with its dynamic structural relations, which is at once simple and complex and which must be holistically grasped if it is to be grasped at all.

When we turn to the distinctive kind of onto-relational order with which we have to reckon in Christian theology, however, we have something else to remember, its profoundly *personal* character. This implies that any approach employing an impersonal model of thought would not be scientifically appropriate or theologically useful, but it does not imply a personalistic approach which operates from a center in the self of the human knower, for that would involve becoming trapped once again in the subject/object relationship and a lapse back into subjectivism. What is theologically required here is some form of personal knowledge similar to that which Michael Polanyi has championed even in the realm of natural science, that is, a responsible participation of the person as an active rational agent in all acts of understanding and knowing, but a participation that is controlled from beyond the knowing person by objective reality and universal standards which transcend his subjectivity.[19] Only a *person* can think, mean, interpret and understand, appraise the validity of an argument or exercise a proper judgment in relating evidence to objective reality; and only a person can discern a coherent pattern in the

reality he is investigating and deploy it as a clue in the active
pursuit of his inquiries. Only a person can freely submit his
mind to the compelling claims of reality upon him, and can
think and decide as he must under obligation to the truth
over which he has no control. In personal knowledge of this
kind, then, a way of knowing is developed, in accordance
with the nature of the realities concerned and through responsible commitment to their authoritative claims, in
which the personal and the objective are fused together in
the activity of establishing contact with reality and its intrinsic rationality.

In Christian theology, personal participation in knowledge is understandably accentuated through the self-communication of God to us in Jesus Christ, which is a personalizing as well as a personal activity. This means that an
intensely personal element characterizes both the object
pole and the subject pole of the onto-relational order in our
knowledge of God. However, we have to take into account
here something more than the establishing of personal reciprocity between God and man, for since it is God as a
Communion of personal Being who communicates himself
to us through Christ and in his Spirit, it is a community of
persons in reciprocity both with God and with one another
that is set up. In other words, the person-constituting interaction of God with us calls into being a church as the
spatiotemporal correlate of his self-giving and self-revealing
to mankind. Correspondingly, the church constitutes the
social coefficient of our knowledge of God, for in the nature
of the case we are unable to know God in any onto-relational way without knowing him in the togetherness of our
personal relations with one another. This is why a realist
evangelical theology that seeks to be rigorously faithful to
the nature of God and his interaction with us in the space
and time of this world cannot but be a church-conditioned
and church-oriented theology. That is part of the scientific

import of Karl Barth's stress upon *church* dogmatics. Yet there is clearly a danger here, lest the subject pole of the knowing relationship should assume a primacy over the object pole of God's self-giving and self-revealing through Christ and in his Spirit. This is why Barth insisted that church dogmatics must be a critical science, for it must constantly bring into question the built-in preconceptions which regulate from behind the church's interpretation of Holy Scripture and formulation of doctrine, for they are too often conditioned by the society and its culture in which the church has taken root. Hence a realist evangelical theology, which in responsible commitment to the nature of God's self-revelation is church-oriented, must seek to engage the church in repentant rethinking of all its interpretation, preaching, and teaching, although the onto-relational character of theology implies that this cannot really be done without a radical renewal of the whole interpersonal life and mission of the church.

Nevertheless, theological science can and should play a basic role in clarifying the nature of its onto-relational subject matter and the distinctive kind of order which it embodies. And it can lead the way forward by penetrating into the intelligible structure of these relations and developing the appropriate modes of conceptuality through which they can be brought to expression and thereby allowed to exert their creative power upon the whole range of human life and thought. Far from schematizing Christian theology into the patterns of the prevailing culture, this should have the opposite effect of transforming the very foundations of culture, thereby creating room within it for the evangelical mission of the church at a level which it has rarely touched except in the great creative periods of Christian thought such as that which spanned the fourth, fifth, and sixth centuries after Christ.

It will be sufficient for us now to focus attention on two

aspects of the theological enterprise in the light of the foregoing discussion.

  a. While there is evidently no way through mere logical analysis or logical construction to understand the ordered field of dynamic onto-relations with which we are concerned in Christian theology, we do have access to the set of conditions within which the distinctive kind of order they embody spontaneously manifests itself, and by indwelling that order we can come up with the anticipatory conceptions or basic clues we need in developing our cognition of it. These conditions are found within the church of Jesus Christ, the worshiping community of God's people. It is there in the midst of the church, its fellowship of love, its meditation upon God's self-revelation through the Holy Scriptures, its Eucharistic life, and its worship of the Father through the Son and in the Spirit, that we become inwardly so adapted to God's interaction with us that we learn, as Origen used to say, how to think *worthily* of God, that is, in a godly way appropriate to God. Just as a child by the age of five has learned an astonishing amount about the physical world to which he has become spontaneously adapted—far more than he could ever understand if he turned out to be the most brilliant of physicists—so we may learn far more than we can ever tell about God within the fellowship of the church, insofar as the church, of course, is genuinely committed to responsible participation in the gospel. It is as within the communion of the Spirit we learn obedience to God's self-giving in Jesus Christ, and instead of being conformed to the cultural patterns of this world are inwardly transformed through a radical change of our mind, that we are able to discern the will of God and acquire the basic insights we need if we are really to develop our knowledge of him in a clear, articulate way. That is to say, within the interpersonal life of the church as the body of Christ and its actualization of corporate reciprocity with God in the space and time of this world, we find not only that we ourselves are personally assimilated into the onto-relational structures that arise, but that our minds become disposed to apprehend God through profoundly intelligible, although nonformalizable (or at least not completely formalizable) relations and structures of thought. We are spiritually and intellectually implicated in patterns of order that are beyond our powers to articulate in explicit terms, but we are aware of being apprehended by divine Truth which steadily presses for increasing realization in our understanding. As far as I can see from the writings of the fathers, that is how classical patristic theology, such as we find coming to expression in the Niceno-Constantinopolitan creed and the conciliar theology that grew out of it, actually developed as it laid the foundations upon which all subsequent Christian theology rests.

It is, I believe, still within the matrix of Eucharistic worship and meditation upon the Holy Scriptures, and evangelical experience in the fellowship and mission of the church, that the empirical and theoretical components in our knowledge of God are found fused together, in a kind of stereoscopic coordination of perceptual and auditive images, and thus provide us with the cognitive instruments we need for explicit theological understanding of God's interaction with us.

b. The kind of scientific theology that arises in this way may be called *fluid dogmatics.* This is not the kind of theology that is developed through logical deduction from fixed premises or axioms, taken from Holy Scripture, or from conciliar or ecclesiastical pronouncements, the typical theology of Roman or Protestant scholasticism, in which statements of the truth tend to be identified in a nominalistic way with the truths they are held to express. Rather, it is the kind of theology that develops under the compelling claims of the Word and Truth of God's self-revelation and their de-

mand for unceasing renewal and reform so that it may be
a theology that serves the Word and Truth of God beyond
itself with increasing fidelity and appropriateness. It is the
kind of dynamic theology which, because it is objectively
oriented in the living God, operates with fluid axioms, i.e.,
axioms that are progressively modified in the light of the
realities that are disclosed to us in God, and which uses them
to penetrate into the intrinsic intelligibility of God's self-
revelation and the structure of the God/world/man or
God/man/world relations which it sets up in space and time
in the history of the people of Israel and supremely in the
incarnation of God's Word and Truth in Jesus Christ. The
deployment of fluid axioms which are continually open to
change and renewal in the light of ever-deeper understanding of God means that the formulations of doctrine organized by reference to them must be *open structures* of thought
and statement. In this event the dogmas that emerge
through the corporate mind of the church in progressive
obedience to the claims of God's Word and Truth upon it
may be likened not to "descriptive" or "explanatory" models, far less to "picturing" models of thought, but to what
are called "disclosure" models of thought. A scientific theory of this kind, even when it attains the status of a physical
law, is rather like a refined lens through which we discern
ontic structures in the universe, or through which we allow
those ontic structures to disclose and interpret themselves to
us. Insofar as that takes place, they are sharply differentiated
from and are relativized by the objective realities which
they serve. In a realist theology this will mean that we must
distinguish no less sharply between dogmatic formulations
of the truth and the truth itself, in the recognition that even
when we have done all that it is our duty to do in relating
them rightly (i.e., in an "orthodox" way) to the truth, they
nevertheless fall far short of what they should be, and are
inadequate. Indeed, it must be said that their inadequacy in

this way is an essential part of their truth, in pointing away from themselves to the truth they serve, as it is an essential element in their objectivity in being grounded beyond themselves on reality that is independent of them.

And so we come back to the point from which we began, the distinction between *theologia nostra* and *theologia in se.*

2.
Theological Questions
to Biblical Scholars

We have been considering the nature and scope of Christian theology as it arises within a complex of relations where the empirical world has a necessary place within the coordinates of our knowledge of God. It is through interaction with this world, in his historical dialogue with Israel and uniquely in the incarnation of his Word in Jesus Christ, that God has made himself known to mankind. And it is within the objectivities and intelligibilities of this world, as they are steadily being disclosed by scientific inquiry, that we are called to respond to God's self-revelation and articulate our knowledge of him. The fact that both theological science and natural science operate within the same structures of space and time that are the bearers of our creaturely rationality implies, as we have seen, that there is a basic area where their different inquiries overlap and where they are open to questioning by each other. Critical epistemological questions are thrust upon us here which a realist theology, in its ontological commitment both to God the Creator and to the world which he has made, may not brush aside, but must allow to have their full force in its own processes of understanding, interpretation, and formulation. Nothing but good can come of entertaining these questions, disturbing as they may be, for they have the effect of cleansing

theology of irrelevant or false concepts and thereby enabling us to be more faithful to the proper ground of God's
self-revelation to us and our knowledge of him.

Our purpose here is not to develop a connected and
constructive argument about biblical interpretation so much
as to clear the ground, by discussing some of these epistemological questions thrown up in the discussion between theology and modern science, and by reflecting on the problems
they raise for biblical interpretation. They are all questions
which I have allowed to be directed to me from the radical
change in the foundations of scientific knowledge, often
with rather devastating effect, but which I pass on to biblical
scholars. They are questions that uncover hidden assumptions and probe into the regulative basis of hermeneutical
activity. While they are not questions as to the material
content of divine revelation or its articulate form in the
Holy Scriptures, they are questions that bear upon the connection between form and content and the relation between
language and things or between words and the realities they
are intended to signify.

The really *fundamental questions* that are thrust upon us
today are those which penetrate to the ultimate assumptions
and regulative beliefs governing all knowledge in the
world, whatever may be the specific field of inquiry in which
we are engaged. Many people today find questions like this
very upsetting, especially if they have been accustomed to
working with the rationalistic contrast between faith and
reason or between belief and demonstration,[1] for they reveal that the persuasive power in argument lies not with our
processes of explicit reasoning, important as they may be,
but with a set of mind or an ultimate belief that arises in us
compulsorily from the ground of our experience in the
universe. It is an ontological act of recognition and assent
which cannot be further analyzed, but without which there
could be no rational or scientific knowledge. Genuinely

ultimate beliefs of this kind are by their nature unprovable and irrefutable, because they have to be assumed in any attempt at proof or disproof and because they involve a relation of thought to being which cannot be put into logical or demonstrable form. Far from being irrational or nonrational, however, ultimate beliefs express the responsible commitment of the mind to reality in which it falls under the power of its intelligible nature and through which it gains the normative insights which prompt and guide our inquiries. As such, ultimate beliefs enable us to interpret our experiences and weigh the evidences of our observations, and direct the reasoning operations of our inquiries to their true ends.

Because these ultimate beliefs constitute the basic framework on which we rely in all rational and scientific activity, they fulfill their function in an informal way as "tacit" coefficients.[2] That is why they are not normally noticed. Indeed one must say that the actual force of their role in regulating our inquiries is often in proportion to our unconscious acceptance of them in the axiomatic principles of our explicit formalizing operations. The more absolute their place in our presuppositions, the less they are brought to our notice in the ordinary course of our science. However, when the advance of knowledge reaches the point where radical change is demanded of us, and fundamental epistemological decisions have to be made, then our ultimate beliefs are forced out into the open. That is to say, we come to the point where we have to put our ultimate beliefs, with which we have been operating as normative assumptions, to the test, in order to determine whether they are genuinely ultimate in the sense that they are forced upon our acknowledgment by the sheer nature and structure of reality or whether they are only substitute beliefs which have misled us and acquired a damaging place in the authoritative principles of our thought. This is what happens when our unquestioned preconceptions begin to show evidence of being in conflict with one another and hidden assumptions are uncovered; it also happens when operative assumptions are found to be at variance with what we are investigating, or when they even prevent us at the very start from giving serious consideration to it. For example, if we work with the assumption that the laws of nature must be timelessly and necessarily true, we cut out any notion of contingence from our understanding of the universe and its rational order; or if we work with a deterministic and mechanistic conception of the universe as a closed continuum of cause and effect, we rule out of scientific explanation right away all the higher intangible levels of human experience and even put forward a completely impersonal view of science from which the human mind is excluded. In this state of affairs a reconstruction of the operative framework of our thought and even of the foundations of knowledge has to take place. Clarification usually reveals the falsity of certain assumptions and the validity of others, and sometimes results in the discovery of new ones, but it results also in a deeper recognition of the all-important role of ultimate beliefs in scientific activitity as essential ingredients deriving from our ontological commitment to the inherent intelligibility of the universe.

This is the situation in which we find ourselves today, for a far-reaching change has been taking place in the framework of knowledge at a level which we have not experienced since the Christian reconstruction of the foundations of knowledge in Greek philosophy, science, and culture in classical patristic times. Age-old assumptions have had to be uprooted and discarded under the compelling pressure of objective reality, and other assumptions have had to be revised or reinforced in their ultimate normative status. Thus the phenomenalist assumption that there is nothing in the mind except what was first in the senses, together with a dualist theory of knowledge in which empir-

ical and theoretical factors are externally connected together, has had to be rejected and a realist, unitary theory
of knowledge in which empirical and theoretical factors are
held to inhere inseparably in one another has taken its place.
At the same time the ultimate belief in the reality and intelligibility of the universe independent of our perceiving and
conceiving of it, together with a profound recognition of its
contingent nature, has been massively reinforced. Moreover, a closer relation of ultimate beliefs to scientific knowledge has come to light, for they are found to be reciprocally
related to the deepening of knowledge and are subject to
constant modification and establishment as under their direction new facts about the universe are discovered and
actual knowledge is advanced.

Since these fundamental changes affect not only natural
scientific knowledge but all our knowledge arising within
the structured intelligibilities of space and time, they call
radically into question not a few of the assumptions which
have controlled modern theological inquiry and biblical
interpretation. That is to say, they call in question the general framework of thought deriving from a phenomenalist
and dualist theory of knowledge. This theory of knowledge,
together with the determinist conception of a closed mechanistic universe to which it gives rise, has the effect of cut-
ting off at the very start any belief in the interaction of God
with the world and with man in the world whereby he
makes himself known in an evidential and conceptual way.
And of course it also has the effect of ruling out of consideration any idea that divine revelation comes to us in an
articulate, verbal, and information-laden form, upon which
our Christian understanding of the Bible rests. If we work
with a set of assumptions antecedently and independently
reached which will not allow us to reckon with a cognitive
relationship to God objectively grounded in the Being of
God himself, and if accordingly we refuse to accept that

what is mediated to us in the Holy Scriptures is epistemically and ontologically grounded in God's own Word, then we are found to interpret the Bible in a radically different way than we would if we rejected that set of assumptions. In actual fact, assumptions of this kind have been rejected by our natural science in its own sphere.

The history of modern science has shown that when we operate with phenomenalist and dualist assumptions of this kind, the observable pattern of things in nature is torn away from a frame of objective structures in reality and loses its underlying coherence, with the result that it suffers serious distortion and disintegration. However, when these assumptions are set aside, a much profounder and more integrated understanding of nature becomes possible in terms of the dynamic field-structures inherent in the ongoing processes of the universe. Hence, for example, as we see in scientific understanding of the fields of radiation that pervade the universe, explanation in terms of mechanical connection has had to give way to explanation in terms of dynamic onto-relations. The implications of this profound reorientation in thought for theological understanding and biblical interpretation are immense, but this does not mean that we may simply switch from one set of controlling assumptions, antecedently and independently reached, to another; for this unitary, integrated way of thinking in which empirical and theoretical factors interpenetrate each other at all levels, demands that our operative assumptions or beliefs must match the distinctive nature and intrinsic intelligibility of the field we are investigating. That is to say, the ultimate beliefs with which we work in Christian theology must be those which press upon us for our recognition and acceptance from the actual ground of God's interaction with us. Hence, instead of being taken over in any unwarranted or uncritical way, they have constantly to be put to the test by reference to the evidential grounds of our deepening

knowledge in theological and hermeneutical activity, so that
they may really measure up to the compelling claims upon
us of God's self-revelation and self-communication to mankind in his historical dialogue with the people of Israel and
in the incarnation of his eternal Word in Jesus Christ. Clarified in this way, however, our ultimate beliefs have a normative function to fulfill which does not conflict with rigorous biblical and theological studies, for they direct the bearing of our inquiries upon reality and thus are essential to the
establishment of knowledge.

Before we go on to discuss the implications of this realist
reorientation of knowledge for biblical interpretation and
to reckon with the questions it poses for current semantics,
let us pause to consider what is meant by *realism*. [3]

The contrast between realism and idealism, implied in the
use of either term, evidently has its source in the distinction
we make between subject and object, idea and reality, or
sign and thing signified. This is a natural operation of the
human mind, for it belongs to the essence of rational behavior that we can distinguish ourselves as knowing subjects
from the objects of our knowledge, and can employ ideas
or words to refer to or signify realities independent of them.
Normally our attention in knowing, speaking, listening, or
reading is not focused upon the ideas or words we use, far
less upon ourselves, but upon the realities they signify or
indicate beyond themselves. Hence in our regular communication with one another we use and interpret signs in the
light of their objective reference. Thus the natural operation of the human mind would appear to be realist.

We use these distinctions, then, between subject and object, idea and reality, or sign and thing signified, naturally
and unreflectingly, and only turn a critical eye upon them
when something arises to obscure signification, such as a
break in the semantic relation. Much now depends upon
where the emphasis falls, upon the signifying pole or the

objective pole of the semantic relation, that is, upon idea or reality, upon sign or thing signified. In this state of affairs the contrast between idealism and realism arises out of an oscillation in emphasis from one pole of the semantic relation to the other. The distinction sharpens into a conflict, however, when the two poles are extended to a breaking point or when the relation between them is disrupted through some dichotomy of thought. However, since the relation between idea and reality or sign and thing signified is never completely severed, there seems to be a regular tendency, as one extreme position is corrected in respect of the other, for each to pass over into the other, so that idealism sometimes passes over into a form of realism and realism passes over into a form of idealism. For example, in the dialectical relation that arises out of a split between theoretical and empirical factors in natural science, an emphasis upon mathematics separated from experience may end up in a mechanical and materialist understanding of the world, while an emphasis upon sense experience as the ultimate ground of knowledge may end up in a rationalist empiricism or even a conventionalism. Virtually the same dialectic arises in theology between radically divergent approaches to the understanding of Christ traditionally characterized as "docetic" and "ebionite," for in modern as in ancient Christologies each tends to turn into a form of the other.[4]

It may be noted that when the semantic relation between idea and reality or between sign and thing signified is not completely severed but only damaged, our thought nevertheless becomes trapped in distorting ambiguities which require correction. It is within the context of this problematic state of affairs, and on the ground of some form of epistemological dualism that underlies it, that coherence and correspondence theories of truth have continually been thrown up in the history of thought. What has always been at stake is a distorting refraction in the ontological substructure of knowledge. The lesson that is constantly being taught is that there can be no satisfactory theory of truth within the brackets of a dualist frame of thought, for it can only yield the oscillating dialectic between coherence and correspondence. There can be no way forward except through a rejection of dualist modes of thought in an integration of empirical and theoretical components in knowledge and of form and being in our understanding of reality. That would restore the integrity of the semantic reference of idea and sign to reality, in which reality would have objective priority over all our conceiving and speaking of it. Strictly speaking, the contrast, let alone the conflict, between realism and idealism would not then arise, nor would the distinction between a coherence and a correspondence view of truth which depends on a disjunction between form and being.

To return to the meaning of *realism,* we shall use the term, not in an attenuated dialectical sense merely in contrast to idealism, nominalism, or conventionalism, but to describe the orientation in thought that obtains in semantics, science, or theology on the basis of a nondualist or unitary relation between the empirical and theoretical ingredients in the structure of the real world and in our knowledge of it. This is an epistemic orientation of the two-way relation between the subject and object poles of thought and speech, in which ontological primacy and control are naturally accorded to reality over all our conceiving and speaking of it. It is worth noting that it was a realist orientation of this kind which Greek patristic theology, especially from the third to the sixth century, struggled hard to acquire and which it built into the foundations of classical theology.[5] Moreover, it is a realist orientation of basically the same kind that we now find restored in the foundations of our empirico-theoretical science, as there have come to light the profound epistemological implications of special and general relativity theory for the unity and continuity of the space-time metrical field in respect of structure and matter/energy, or form and dynamic being, at all levels of reality throughout the contingent universe.

However, the general position that has prevailed in Western thought in medieval and modern times has been thoroughly dualist owing to the immense impact of Augustinian-Aristotelian and Augustinian-Newtonian frames of thought upon our science, philosophy, and theology. Nowhere, perhaps, have dualist modes of thought been more deeply entrenched in our cultural tradition than in our understanding of *language,* whether in its relation to the society in which it grows and takes shape or in its relation to our environment in the space-time world in which we live, speak, and think, and which provides the common objective medium for our public communication with one another today as well as for historical communication across the centuries. All this has undoubtedly affected people's understanding of the language of the Bible—as indeed it was bound to do—so that the dialectic arising out of a damaged semantic relation has in one way or another left its deep imprint upon modern biblical scholarship, as one can see very clearly in the familiar contraposition between fundamentalist and conventionalist approaches to the Holy Scriptures. It is, then, to this area that we must now give specific attention, so that we may bring to bear upon it the critical questions that arise out of the realist orientation in thought which we have been discussing, and thus clear the way for a more natural interpretation of the biblical message.

1. QUESTIONS ABOUT THE FUNCTION OF LANGUAGE
We may begin by considering the invention of symbolic systems or highly formalized "languages," which is one of the outstanding features of rigorous science today. Contrary

to what might at first appear, as we have already seen, this
is not intended to be a flight into abstraction but is a way
of refining and developing the natural operation of the
mind in its realist use of language. Symbolic systems of this
kind are formal instruments of thought enabling us to cope
more adequately with the world of our actual experience by
extending the range and power of our thought beyond what
we would be capable of without them. Symbolic or formal
systems are not invented for their own sake, but are used to
deepen and widen the bearing of our thought upon empirical reality and to enable us to grasp its intrinsic intelligibilities at a deeper level. In order to perform that function they
have constantly to be purified and refined so that they may
become more and more apposite ways of representing the
structured objectivities of the universe as these become disclosed through our inquiries. Everything goes wrong, however, if the formal language does not prove to be an apposite system of representation, or if the relation between the
symbols we employ and the realities upon which they are
meant to bear is damaged, for then the symbolic systems
break loose from the objective control of reality and bear
upon it only in an indirect, ambiguous, and misleading way.
The problem is complicated, however, by the fact that symbolic systems cannot be used on their own but only along
with a verbal language, and by the fact that verbal language
has widely come to be understood as a way of self-expression on the part of the subject using it or of the society to
which he and his language belong.[6]

Attention has been directed to these difficulties mainly by
mathematicians and mathematical physicists who have been
forced, in the interests of rigor, to examine the relation
between number language (or symbolic language) and
word language. The symbolic systems developed by the
mathematicians (different geometries or algebras, for example) can be used only in coordination with some other lan-

guage such as English, German, or French, but modern attitudes to language have distorting effects on mathematical representation. How is word language to be coordinated with number language in such a way that it may serve the objective of a mathematical science?

Any answer to this question requires of us some discussion of the relation between language and thought and language and things, to which we shall turn shortly. In the meantime, it may be pointed out that normally we think things through language and through the ideas it expresses. The intention of our thought does not terminate properly on ideas, far less on words or statements, but on things we intend through them. The difficulty is that ordinary language, wherever we find it, is already a deposit of residual epistemologies and philosophies, especially a language that is bound up with a high and long cultural tradition. Language of this kind is full of analogies and images which arise out of society and it is geared into the paradigms of its cultural tradition. Thus when we have to coordinate language with the technical representations of extremely difficult and exact inquiries of science, language can prove an opaque medium and get in the way through its distorting effects. Hence the coordination of word language with number language has to be developed in such a way that we do not read the latent images or analogies in word language back into the material content of scientific knowledge. This involves the discipline of thinking in such a way that, through highly refined symbolic or formal structures, images are made to refer imagelessly to the realities intended. Imageless reference of this kind is of particular importance in relativity and quantum theory, where we must beware of projecting visual images into the realities we apprehend, for as often as not they are intrinsically invisible.

Here we have an understanding of the function of language which conflicts rather sharply with that which seems to prevail widely in contemporary biblical scholarship, which is still tied up with an observationalist and phenomenalist approach—that is, with knowledge and interpretation of things in accordance with the way they appear to people rather than in accordance with their intrinsic relations and structures. Hence biblical scholars are too apt to treat the language of biblical documents in terms of its subjective reference or social matrix, that is, as primarily expressing the subjects of the authors or the mind of the community in which the documents arose. Thus it is not surprising that they opt for some interpretation in terms of an indirect or oblique reference uncontrolled by objective reality, with the result that one rather unnatural and artificial interpretation seems to replace another as scholar follows upon scholar.

While modern biblical scholarship in spite of these methods has certainly contributed a great deal to our understanding of the Scriptures from various points of view, it is nevertheless clear that its basic understanding of the function of language must now be called in question together with the dualist approach from which it derives. The chief lessons to be learned in this respect concern the objective orientation of language which we naturally and properly use as a *transparent medium* of representation in the process of knowing and speaking about realities in terms of their own intrinsic significance.[7] It is thus the direct rather than the oblique intention that is primary, so that understanding and interpretation of the Scriptures does not focus myopically, as it were, upon the words and statements themselves, but *through* them on the truths and realities they indicate beyond themselves. It is in the light of that semantic function that the words and statements themselves are properly understood, for their real meaning lies not in themselves but in what they intend. Regarded in this way, the Holy Scriptures are the *spectacles* through which we are brought to know the true God in such a way that our minds fall under the compelling power of his self-evidencing Reality.[8]

2. QUESTIONS ABOUT THE RELATION OF LANGUAGE TO THINGS

Fundamental questions about the relationship of language to things were once raised by Plato in the *Cratylus* in a discussion about the basis of language.[9] Do the terms (or "names," *onomata*) we use have their significance in virtue of some natural relation *(physei)* between them as verbal signs and the realities they signify, or simply in virtue of an extrinsic conventional *(nomō, thesei)* relation? Plato argued that if the words or verbal signs we use are only artificially related through convention or custom to the realities for which they are claimed to stand, or if they are so completely detached that they have no natural bearing on these realities, then they are empty of real significance and semantically useless, and all grounds for raising questions about the truth or falsity of statements is removed. On the other hand, if words or verbal signs are so completely adequate in their representation of the realities they stand for that they substitute for them, or if they image the realities they signify so closely as to be indistinguishable from them, they will be mistaken for the realities concerned and fail in their function as significant signs. Hence if words or signs are to do their job properly, they must have some measure of detachment or incompleteness or even discrepancy to allow them to point away from themselves to the realities intended, in the light of which their truth or falsity will be judged. Words and statements must be related to the realities of things they are intended to signify in such a way that the realities "show through," or manifest themselves through them, and yet in such a way that knowledge of those realities cannot be read off language, for they are independent of the language used to indicate them. That is to say, words and statements are understood only when we come to know *through* them what is being indicated *apart from* them.[10]

The significance of this for our immediate concern here can be brought out by expressing it in this way. A realist position is one in which signs are naturally correlated to, and are ontologically controlled by, the realities they signify, *but* when signs and realities signified perfectly coincide, or when statements are absolutely adequate to their objects, so that they substitute for them or are mistaken for them, then an ultra-realist position is set up which tumbles over into its dialectical opposite, some form of nominalism or conventionalism. This is what takes place when a statement about the truth is identified with the truth itself, or when the truth of statement is identified in our thought with the truth of being. A genuinely realist position, therefore, will be one in which the sign differentiates itself as a sign from the reality on which it bears, therein revealing a measure of disparateness or discrepancy which is essential to its successful functioning as a sign. For a true statement to serve the truth of being, it must fall short of it, be revisable in the light of it, and not be mistaken for it, since it does not possess its truth in itself but in the reality it serves. Thus a dash of inadequacy is necessary for its precision.

Now this is precisely the understanding of the relation of language to things which the realist reorientation in scientific knowledge has been bringing back. This is very evident in the operation of relativity theory, when mathematical representation of an invariant relatedness inherent in the universe bears upon it in such a way that that objective relatedness confers relativity upon every representation of it.[11] That is to say, all our theoretical statements fall short of the reality they indicate and are constantly revisable in the light of it. This is also evident in the general scientific demand to distinguish public language from private language, by correlating our use of language to the constant physical medium of the world around us. Otherwise, grounds for universal validity in scientific statements are removed. Apart from the ontological reference of language to reality independent of it, there are no grounds for raising questions as to the truth or falsity of our concepts, and the essential objective of scientific inquiry, as Einstein expressed it, "grasping the real in all its depth,"[12] becomes impossible to achieve.

If the ontological reference of scientific theories is damaged or rejected, two fatal errors set in which undermine the foundations of knowledge: "operationalism" and "formalism." Operationalism is the pragmatic approach to scientific knowledge as a way of organizing our experiences in an operationally effective manner. Consequently it regards scientific theories not as theories having an independent cognitive function, or as interpretative instruments giving access to otherwise inaccessible truth, but as no more than convenient arrangements of our observational data, mere working hypotheses, which have no bearing upon being or reality. Formalism, on the other hand, represents the abstract theoretical approach to scientific knowledge in which real connections are replaced by symbolic or formal connections detached from the control of objective reality. Consequently scientific theories become little more than empty conceptual schemata invested with a prescriptive role in determining our understanding of nature under a misguided conception of truth as that which can be reduced to logically exact and completely formalized relations.

Both operationalism and formalism collapse within the realist reorientation of scientific knowledge of which we have been speaking, but their rejection by science poses severely critical questions to their counterparts frequently found in modern biblical scholarship: "subjectivist existentialism" and "linguistic formalism." Existentialist exegesis is a way of interpreting biblical documents by using them as a foil to enable the human subject to take up a position in the universe consonant with his own self-understanding in such a way that the universe of things and people becomes meaningful for him. On the other hand, linguistic exegesis of a severely syntactical and logicist kind is a way of interpreting the biblical documents as the source for propositional truths which can be organized in strictly formalized patterns of thought and which are regarded as having certainty and authority in themselves apart from subjection to the critical control of self-evidencing reality in God independent of them. However, in the light of the critical questions directed at them by a realist science, subjectivist existentialism and linguistic formalism are both found to be ultimately nonsensical, for they are little more than a mere game we play, with ourselves or with words and statements. The existentialist handling of biblical language appears to be an obscurantist retreat from the given fabric of the created universe of space and time within which alone God makes himself known to us, and thus it appears to empty Christian faith of any objective or evidential ground or any conceptual content of its own. And the formalistic treatment of biblical language appears to be a rationalist detachment of the Scriptures from the objective truth of God independent of them, an approach in which it is assumed that biblical statements contain their truth and evidence wholly in themselves in their syntactical relations, so that they are capable of being elaborated in a flat fundamentalist way into logically consistent structures and prescriptive systems of thought which stand upon themselves.

The basic lesson which we must surely learn today in biblical scholarship, in the light of a realist relation between language and things, is that real understanding arises where biblical statements refer us to what is true independently of them, so that in a profound sense genuine understanding begins where biblical statements leave off.[13] This requires from us a basically *theological* exegesis and interpretation of the Bible, in which we learn to understand what it says through its function in mediating to us knowledge of divine truths which are what they are independently of the Bible. These are truths which we must think out—while certainly on the basis of the biblical revelation—in terms of conceptual forms that arise as they press for recognition and realization in our minds. We apprehend and understand them as we submit our minds to their informing power and self-evidencing reality.

In view of this need for an objectively grounded conceptuality in theological interpretation of biblical language, we recall the point discussed in the first chapter about the interpenetration of observational and conceptual images at all levels of our experience, which applies no less strongly here. So far we have been considering in this chapter the relation of signs to things signified by them, but what of the relation of *ideas* to the realities they signify in their own conceptual way? This raises another problem for biblical and theological interpretation which must be clarified before we proceed further. This concerns the fact that from time to time in the history of hermeneutical activity an underlying dualism has had a divisive effect upon the signifying sign, splitting it into an outer sensible aspect and an inner intelligible aspect, i.e., into form and content. In this event the two-tier relation between sign and thing has been replaced by a three-tier relation between sign, significate, and thing. The significate, which intervenes between the sign and the thing signified, is the conceptual content of the sign by means of which or through which, as an ideal form or conceptual sign, reference is made to the object or thing conceived. This mode of indirect reference to reality almost always gives rise to substitute ontology (or phenomenology). Since the significate is held to be what is immediately signified by the sign, it tends to stand for or replace the

objective reality in our thought, and thus takes on an objec-
tified status itself. It is frequently in this objectification of
ideal forms, i.e., into conceptual "realities," that idealism
arises. Here the dialectic, which we noted earlier, comes
into play. Insofar as this idealism leans toward objective
reality it can become a form of realism, but insofar as it leans
toward the conceptual content as what is signified, it can
become a form of conceptualism or even tumble into nominalism. It is within the context of this problematic state of
affairs that we find regularly emerging the subtle identification of conceptual representation of the truth with the truth
itself, or of the truth of statement with the truth of being.
It is this identification of the conceptual significate with the
reality signified, rather than an outright identity of verbal
sign and reality signified, that is so characteristic of fundamentalist interpretation of the Bible. This is certainly understandable within the context of the Augustinian-Newtonian
framework of thought with which Protestant fundamentalism usually operates, and it is for that very reason that
fundamentalism often feels so threatened by a genuinely
realist science—one which respects the integrity of the consistent structure of the contingent universe—and tends instead to find justification for its approach in a rather nominalist conception of scientific method. This can only bring
fundamentalism into deeper conflict with scientific or theological realism, in accordance with which reality itself must
be allowed to be the ultimate judge of the rightness or
wrongness, the truth or falsity, of our concepts of it.[14]

It is certainly clear that in any serious theological study of
the Holy Scriptures we cannot operate without concepts,
but since they have to be natural to the material content of
God's self-revelation to us in and through the Scriptures, we
have to develop them as we go along and work them into
an interpretative framework for continuously deepening exegesis and interpretation. As such, however, they must be

constantly submitted to critical clarification and revision in the light of the realities that become disclosed to us through the Scriptures, so that they may retain their semantic function as conceptual signs and not become theological objects which terminate our understanding on themselves. That is to say, instead of being objectifications of the truth, our concepts are to be transparent, open structures of thought, forged under the impact of divine revelation in the Scriptures, structures through which the Truth of God is allowed to disclose itself to us in ways appropriate to it and through which, therefore, our deepening understanding of him terminates on God himself and not upon conceptual significates or propositional ideas.

3. QUESTIONS ABOUT THE RELATION OF LANGUAGE TO CONNECTION

Here we have a serious problem to which we have given far too little attention in spite of the fact that Alfred North Whitehead, among others, kept on pointing out that it requires solution if we are to match our scientific thinking and our linguistic expression adequately to one another.[15] It is of the very essence of scientific activity that we think connections, or think things in their relations and interrelations with one another, and indeed, as we do today, develop dynamic and relational theories to account for the onto-relations which characterize the real world of space and time. We have to express these relations in language, number language and word language, but the kind of relations inherent in these languages may be very different from the kind of relation with which we are concerned in the field of our inquiry. For example, in biological investigations we try to grasp and account for morphological relations which we cannot bring to adequate expression in our linear mathematical equations. The difficulty is just as great, if not so apparent, in our employment of word language, for again and again we have to grapple with relations which conflict with the syntactical connections in the language we use. This is especially the case, Whitehead used to insist, with our classical Aryan languages that are built upon the model of subject-predicate relations which have a tendency to distort the kind of connections we want to express. Thus instead of adapting our language to make it more appropriate, we insist on casting our discoveries into linguistic molds that can only obscure and obstruct our appreciation of them.[16]

Newton's struggle to give mathematical expression to the universe of bodies in motion is highly instructive here. On the one hand he was forced to invent fluxions, or what we call the differential calculus, to give a scientifically tractable account of the kind of dynamic relation or motion we find in the trajectory of a cannonball, but on the other hand he gave systematic expression to a universe governed by the laws of motion by recourse to Euclidean geometry which is the geometry of rigid relations independent of time, so that he tended to impose upon his "system of the world" an artificial, abstract distortion. In more recent times mathematical scientists have had to elaborate new geometries and new algebras, not only to cope with Newton's problems but to cope with the more subtle kinds of connection that emerge in relativity and quantum theory.

Part of the difficulty, of course, lies in the fact that our traditional mathematics have been developed within the matrix of cultures and their languages which have left an imprint upon them that now brings them into conflict with the kind of relations that are now being disclosed through our empirico-theoretical inquiries.[17] We cannot go into those problems here, but sufficient has been said to indicate that serious questions about the relation of language to connection are increasingly being put to us which must not be brushed aside in any serious concern with biblical language. Nor is this the place to discuss how these languages of ours may be modified or adapted to make them more appropriate to the task to which we want to put them, but at least we may learn to beware of corrupting what we apprehend of God's interaction with us from his self-revelation in the Holy Scriptures by the way we use language in bringing it to theological expression and formulation. Unless we watch ourselves very carefully in biblical interpretation we may well distort everything right from the start, through being trapped in alien linguistic forms.

There is a cognate question here to which we must give attention, namely, the question as to whether we are not often guilty of trying to put into linguistic form the relation of language to being, or the relation of words and sentences to the things they signify, which is quite impossible. Just as we are unable to picture how a picture pictures a landscape, so we are unable to put into statements how statements bear upon being. If we attempted to do so, we would only convert the relation that obtains between statement and being into another kind of relation altogether, that which obtains between statement and statement. That would be the disastrous mistake of converting semantic relations without remainder into syntactical relations, which is a widespread failing in modern biblical scholarship.[18] Let us grant to Whitehead that the kind of syntax with which we operate in our traditional languages in the West, especially those which have been deeply influenced by Greek and Latin, presents real difficulties for us in theological as in scientific formulation. They are not difficulties that we can finally avoid so long as we use these languages, but at least we can take care not to let our thought be trapped in syntactical relations through falling into the common mistake noted above, that is, by reducing all semantic relations into syntactic relations. Certainly the Gödelian theorems—which we may transpose from a logico-deductive system to a grammatico-syntactic or a logico-syntactic system—warn us that *no syntactics contains its own semantics.* [19] That is to say, the referential relations of language must be given priority over syntactical relations, while it is only as syntactical relations are themselves open through their boundary conditions to a controlling center beyond them that they may be meaningfully understood themselves. If syntactical relations can be understood and handled in this way, it is not so likely that we will project the kind of relations that obtain among words and sentences into the objective realities to which they are semantically correlated.

In view of this discussion two suggestions may be offered to biblical scholars. First, in order to avoid imposing later technical developments upon the Bible and to reach a more natural interpretation of its language, it would be helpful to work with the understanding and use of language that obtained before the age of syntactical dominance to which the elaboration of formal grammars and dictionaries has contributed so heavily. Second, in order to avoid linguistic reductionism, care should be taken to preserve the different levels of connection intact by treating the kind of connections found at one level as the limiting case of another which may be handled as a meta-level. Coordination of different levels of connection in this cross-level way will go far toward clarifying the semantic focus of the biblical documents in which biblical and theological thinking are harnessed together.

4. QUESTIONS ABOUT THE PHONETIC CHARACTER OF LANGUAGE

There is an interesting passage in Plato's *Phaedrus* in which he discusses the propriety and superiority of the spoken over the written word, and points to the fact that the reduction of what is spoken to writing actually creates forgetfulness, for it is an aid to reminiscence, not to the memory—and what is more, it does not set before the reader the truth itself but only the semblance of the truth.[20] This helps us to understand why Plato insisted on retaining the dialogical form in his own writings, for it is through that kind of interaction between speaker and hearer that confrontation with truth arises so that the word intended is conveyed through the interchange in thought and speech that takes place between the partners in the dialogue. That is to say, the response evoked by the word is assimilated into what the word communicated is meant to be. Here, as so often, Plato puts his finger upon a very significant point, one which, with the application of electronics to the study of language, our scientific research has been recovering. This relates to the difference, to use Whitehead's expressions, between the basically natural "language of sound" and the relatively artificial "language of sight."[21] Of course there can be no doubt about the immeasurable importance of the invention of writing and its use in the progress of civilization at all levels, but the elaboration of literary form in sophisticated cultures has also had the effect of overlaying and obscuring the natural character and dynamic structure of language in its live form.

In this state of affairs it would seem that a fresh appreciation of sound-language has the effect of making us unthink many of our unquestioned assumptions, not least those which have entrenched themselves unawares in our minds since the invention of movable type and the proliferation of printed books and which have been affected by the phenomenalist and observationalist outlook that has dominated Western culture since Galileo and Newton. A rampant *visualization and spatialization of language* has set in which has had the effect of intensifying what John Macmurray, Martin Buber, and others have called the opticizing of thought—thinking with our eyes—which is bound to be somewhat superficial, since sight cannot penetrate into the interior structure of things.[22] Nor indeed can sight cope with dynamic connections. This creates serious problems for knowledge, as quickly became clear in the empiricist approaches of John Locke and David Hume, who insisted on restricting rational and scientific thought to demonstrations operating only with "visible certain connections," thereby denigrating invisible, intangible, not to speak of time-related, connections. This visualization and spatialization of language, and the linking of thought to language affected in this way, together with the inability of human sight to cope with movement except at low velocities (when space and time are split apart), have created serious problems for physics. Hence some physicists have called for sound-based concepts to help out the articulation of empirico-theoretical connections which we cannot do adequately with sight-based concepts and their corresponding linguistic expression,[23] and others have been calling for relational modes of thought and speech derived from non-European cultures and languages in order to give adequate and appropriate expression to the dynamic ontic relations and coherences embedded in nature.[24]

It is above all in theological science in which our knowledge is grounded upon the Word of God—that is, as Hilary once expressed it, "the might of his uttered voice"[25]—that we need, if not sound-based, at least word-based concepts, which elsewhere I have called *audits*. [26] We have to reckon with the fact that in the Greek tradition of thought *idea,* as its derivation makes clear, is a mode of vision—and with the fact that in the Latin tradition of thought there is no term corresponding to hearing as *percept* corresponds to perceiving and *concept* corresponds to conceiving, with the result that in Latin-related languages we are tempted to construe knowledge that comes through hearing regularly and distortingly in terms of percepts and concepts alone. That brings home to us the fact that a serious theology rooted in the Word of God, mediated to us articulately through the language of the Holy Scriptures in which we hear "God speaking in person,"[27] requires us to develop apposite modes of thought and speech both in interpretation of the Bible and in constructive theological formulation. This became evident even in the Latin theology of the Middle Ages, when Anselm claimed that since knowledge of God rests ultimately upon a speaking inherent in his very Being *(locutio apud Summam Substantiam),* in order to understand biblical and theological statements we have to *listen in* to the truth to which they refer us in God. Understanding *(intelligere)* was held to be a form of inward reading *(intus-legere)* and to be controlled by an underlying act of audition *(subauditio)* in which we constantly give ear to God's Truth.[28] Similarly at the end of the Middle Ages attempts were made to bring vision and audition in our understanding of God together, as in expressions like "intuitive audition" or "auditive intuition" which we find in the writings of John Major, one of John Calvin's teachers in the University of Paris.[29] These are precisely the issues which after the Reformation a Latin-based theology, such as that of John of the Cross, again sought to take with the utmost seriousness in replacing a model of vision by a model of hearing in an account of the knowledge of God.[30] However, it is in the high Reformation theology of the Word, advocated above all by Luther and Calvin and revived in a massive way by Karl Barth, that we find a way of interpreting the language and statements of the Bible and formulating Christian doctrine through an attempt to restore the connection between the Word written and the Word spoken, and therefore within the ongoing proclamation and mission of "the hearing and teaching church" (the *ecclesia audiens et docens*).[31] It is still over these issues, together with those thrown up by an underlying dualist epistemology, that the sharpest clash is to be found among the ranks of biblical scholars.

The questions which this new appreciation of the *phonetic*

character of language poses for biblical scholarship become very pointed when we turn to the modern obsession with the analysis of linguistic and literary form. They are questions whether we are not apt to distort the natural character of biblical language and the basic genre of its literary form through analytical distinctions that make them conform to alien patterns of thought. Some of these questions may be listed, and their implications considered.

a. There is a question as to the relation between the observational and the auditive form. Does not modern biblical criticism operate with a disruption of the natural inherence of vision and hearing, due to presuppositions trapped within the sound/sight split of what Newton used to call "the sensorium"? It is to be granted that biblical revelation has come down to us in the form of written documents, but these documents cannot be torn out of the historical dialogue of God with his people, or therefore out of the oral tradition of divine revelation through Israel and the apostolic foundation of the church in Jesus Christ, without having their natural ostensive meaning undermined.

b. Another question concerns the relation of language to memory. This is one of the questions already raised by Plato, but it is now rather more pressing. Does the way of thinking which gives primacy to written language not operate with a different organization of recall, on a linear, word-for-word basis, rather than with one employing in-depth structures which characterize the natural memory or the ongoing informal, tacit coefficient of explicit thought? In other words, the memory bank of oral tradition and dialogical communication is not organized along digital lines. If therefore we are unable to conceive free recall of great masses of material such as we have in the Gospels as from the mouth of Jesus, that does not give us leave to insist that most of this material is the free creation of the early Christian community.

c. A further question concerns the relation of language to time. Modern science has certainly raised problems for us in the sound/sight relation, for sound requires a medium for its propagation as light does not, but that reinforces the point that sound-language is more intimately bound up with the life and history of interpersonal communication. On the other hand, the fact that time relations are found to inhere in the ongoing processes of contingent reality means that we can no longer operate with the split between absolute, geometrical time and relative, phenomenal or sensible time, which gave rise to the disastrous distinction between *Historie* and *Geschichte* which has prevailed in and distorted biblical interpretation in this century.[32]

d. There is also a question concerning the relation of language to space. This is a question as to whether modern biblical scholarship is not still tied to impossible, pseudo-scientific notions. The problems go back to the Greek receptacle and container notions of space that had become embedded in Greco-Roman culture, with which the biblical message of God's interaction with mankind, and not least of the incarnation of his eternal Word, in space and time, came into sharp conflict. Classical Christian theology had to work out a radically relational view of space, as well as time, in the light of the interrelation it found between the doctrines of incarnation and creation; otherwise, it found quite alien patterns of thought being clamped down upon the understanding of the Bible.[33] In modern times, however, these problems have been greatly reinforced by the fact that Newtonian science built a container notion of space into the fabric of Western science and culture.[34] While that has certainly been overthrown by relativity theory so far as pure science is concerned, it still retains a powerful hold on the popular mind and on biblical scholarship. This is very evident, for example, in the way in which Bultmann has deployed the spurious notion of a "three-decker universe" in his exegesis of biblical language and in his attempt to cut faith in Jesus Christ completely away from the structures of space and time, in which, of course, he makes use of the no less spurious conception of two kinds of "history."[35] The most widespread difficulty, however, comes from the subtle spatialization of biblical language, which demands a phenomenalist and observationalist approach, and which has the effect of undermining the auditive character of biblical language and subjecting it to interpretation of visual images and myths. Another result of the spatialization of biblical language is found in the way in which many people, preachers and scholars alike, who want to take seriously the relation of the Holy Scriptures to the Word of God nevertheless think of the Word of God as *contained* in the Bible, which imports into their interpretation of the Bible a strangely damaging understanding of the relation of form and content, and leads to the nominalist identification of biblical statements with the truths to which they refer.

To point up the relevance of these issues for modern biblical scholarship, let us consider the historico-critical analysis of the Gospels. How much does our approach to the Synoptic problem and to the documentary hypothesis (the document Q, for example), depend on criteria which we derive from the determination of literary form, and which we use in determining the oral form that preceded the composing of the Gospels in the form in which they have come down to us? So far as I can see, form criticism and redaction criticism alike work with the discarded assumptions of observationalism and phenomenalism. Thus they assume that theoretical elements can only have a later origin and have to be put down to the creative spirituality of the early Christian community rather than to Jesus himself. Thus they disrupt the way in which the empirical and theological elements (for example, in the parables of Jesus and their interpretation) are already coordinated in the evangelical tradition, but since this takes away from the Gospel presentation of Christ its underlying coherence, different conceptual patterns have to be brought in, allegedly from the self-understanding of the early Christian community, to tie what remains of the traditional material together. A similar problem arises when literary forms, phenomenologically detached from the event-situations in which they are embedded in the Gospels, are conceptualized through assimilation to the alleged patterns of consciousness in the Christian community, and then new event-situations have to be thought up for them in the community in order to make the reconstruction seem plausible. This is the kind of occasion in traditiohistorical criticism when it is apparently useful to have two different conceptions of history, one to show that the event-situation recorded by the Evangelists is historically impossible and must have been invented by them, and another to justify the hypothetical event-situation in the community as existentially meaningful. This only serves to show how on a dualist basis of thought it is rather easy to bend the evidence to suit what we want to make of it, or at least to fit it into our preconceived framework of thought.

Here we evidently have at work in modern biblical scholarship the constructivist rationalism with which we are familiar elsewhere in the history of phenomenalist thought in the ambiguous game of piecing together what has already disintegrated through its basic assumptions and analytical methods, so that one artificially contrived framework after another has to be thought up in order to "save the appearances." Behind this, however, lies what F. A. Hayek in another connection has called the *Synoptic delusion,* that is, the fiction that enough can be known of all the relevant facts to make such a reconstruction.[36] Apart from straining the demands of credulity beyond anything that we have in the Evangelists' presentation of Jesus and his teaching, however, this approach evidently asks us to believe either that the Evangelists were unable to distinguish between truth and falsity or that they deliberately set about misrepresenting what took place and reinterpreting what Jesus had said to suit purposes of their own—both of which are quite preposterous. Michael Dummett has expressed his own sharp critique in this way:

> The appeals made in current Biblical exegesis to the principle of literary forms pays no attention to the demands of credibility: they have become a mere technique for enabling the exegete, without formally denying the truthfulness of the Biblical writers, to believe the same as any critic uncommitted to their truthfulness. Thus, for example, it is common to say that the explanation of the parable of the sower which the synoptic Gospels represent our Lord as giving was not his, and does not reflect the interpretation which he intended, but is, rather, an adaptation of the parable to the situation of the early Church. If you see no reason to avoid imputing to the evangelists an attempt to give a spurious authority to a reinterpretation of the parable, you may find this convincing.[37]

How would any rigorous science react to the fact that some theoretical approach to account for a baffling set of events had persistently broken down, in spite of a thousand modifications to make it successful in achieving its objective in a convincing explanation? The one compelling scientific conclusion would be the utter inadequacy or the impossibility of the enterprise, even though many new facts had been brought to light as by-products in the long story of its falsification. That is what has happened to the phenomenalist and observationalist approach to the quest of the historical Jesus over a hundred and fifty years of historico-critical research. In spite of a thousand modifications when almost every new scholar, especially if he is German, comes up with a new slant to the quest, and in spite of the fact that we have learned an immense amount about the Bible, its language and its message, we are nevertheless no further forward to our objective along that road, for the historical Jesus keeps on eluding us.[38] The time has long since overtaken us when we have to face squarely and honestly scientific questions as to the adequacy of our analytical methods, the modes of our thinking, the linguistic instruments we have been using, and behind them all questions as to the controlling assumptions and beliefs we have accepted. This is not to agree that research into the historical Jesus Christ is impossible, but rather to say that it cannot be carried out in the way it has been attempted or with the methods it has used for so long. A profound reorientation in our approach and in our historico-critical research is needed, a reorientation of a realist kind, in which dualist assumptions and abstractions are set aside so that as we proceed we may be free to develop appropriate methods of interpretation and theological construction—under the control of regulative beliefs which derive from the articulate self-revelation of God in his own Word and Truth as they have become incarnate in Jesus Christ. In him we are confronted with the ultimate Reality of God which must be accepted or rejected on its own ground, for it cannot be verified or validated on any other ground than that which it provides itself. It is then in the context of that interaction of God with us in Jesus Christ that Jesus Christ himself is to be understood and the Gospels are to be interpreted, yet in such a way that we do not retreat from the given fabric of the space-time universe which God has made, or from the created objectivities and intelligibilities within which the incarnation took place.

3.
A Realist Interpretation
of God's Self-Revelation

We have considered the fact that Christian theology arises within and is bounded by a triadic relation in which God, man, and world are involved together in a movement of God's personal and creative interaction with man whereby he makes himself known to him within the objectivities and intelligibilities of the empirical world. We have also considered the fact that if we abandon a phenomenalist and observationalist theory of knowledge and its damaging bifurcation between sign and reality signified and between form and content, we return to a more natural and realist view of signification and communication in which language is used and understood through its semantic function in objective reference to realities independent of it. We have now to focus our attention on the self-revelation of God to man through his historical dialogue with the people of Israel and in the incarnation of his Word and Truth in Jesus Christ, which gave rise to the Holy Scriptures of the Old and New Testaments. It is thus a Bible-related revelation of God that we must have in view and seek to interpret, for it is in that articulate form of human word, spoken and written, which divine revelation has taken in space and time, that God continues to make himself known to us as we meditate upon the Holy Scriptures and hear his Word addressing us.

By revelation is meant, then, not some vague, inarticulate awareness of God projected out of the human consciousness, but an intelligible, articulate revealing of God by God whom we are enabled to apprehend through the creative power of his Word addressed to us, yet a revealing of God by God which is actualized within the conditions of our creaturely existence and therefore within the medium of our human thought and speech.[1] This is a self-revelation of God which posits and sustains man as the partner of its full movement from God to man and from man back to God. There is created such a profound reciprocity between God and man that in assuming human form, divine revelation summons an answering movement from man toward God, which is taken up into the movement of revelation as a constitutive ingredient in God's revelation of himself to man.[2] Thus the articulate self-communication of God to man includes within itself meeting between man and God as well as between God and man, for in assuming the form of human speech and writing the revelation of God addressed to man becomes at the same time the obedient response of man to God whereby revelation is anchored and realized in the conditions of human reality as well as divine Reality.

It is, of course, in the revelation of God actualized in our historical human existence through the instrumentality of Israel and in Jesus Christ the Word made flesh in Israel, in whom that actualization of divine revelation was brought to its fulfillment in acutely personalized form, that we learn about this self-revelation of God and the response of man. We do not derive it from a phenomenological analysis of the life situations of ancient Israel as recorded in the Old Testament writings or the life situations of the apostolic church as recorded in the New Testament writings. It comes directly from the revealing activity of the Word of God who as the creative source of human being has penetrated

through the barriers of estrangement, opened it out to the
light and understanding of God, and established a two-way
connection between God and man in the incarnation where
the human response is faithful and true to the divine revelation and not in the last analysis just a refracted form of man's
self-understanding. This is Jesus Christ, the Interpreter and
Mediator between man and God, who as God and man
constitutes in the unity of his incarnate Person the divine-
human Word spoken to man from the highest and heard by
him in the depths, and spoken to God out of the depths and
heard by him in the highest. He is not only the Word of
God come to man and become man, but he who as man
bears and is the Word of God, the Word not only as God
speaks it but the same Word as heard, spoken, and lived by
man. As such Jesus Christ is the Word through whom and
with whom and in whom the true and faithful response of
man is made to God and divine revelation completes the
circle of its own movement.[3]

Before we pursue this further, let us note that the reciprocity created by God's revelation of himself to man takes
a corporate form. In order to be heard and understood, and
to be communicable as Word, divine revelation penetrates
into the speaker-hearer relationship within the interpersonal structure of humanity and becomes speech to man by
becoming speech of man to man, spoken and heard through
the intelligible medium of a people's language. Thus the
reciprocity created by the movement of divine revelation
takes the form of a community of reciprocity between God
and man established in human society, which then under the
continuing impact of divine revelation becomes the appropriate medium of its continuing communication to man.

That is what took place in God's dialogue with Israel, for
God's revelation of himself to mankind did not operate in
a vacuum, but penetrated into human existence in the particular life and history of one people elected as the instrument

for the actualization of God's revelation in humanity and separated as a holy nation in whose midst God dwelt in an intimate and distinctive way through the presence of his Word. In the covenanted relationship thus set up between Israel and God, Israel found itself a people invaded by divine revelation and progressively subjected to its molding and informing power in such a way that the responses which divine revelation provoked from it, whether of obedience or disobedience, enlightenment or blindness, were made instruments for its deepening penetration into its existence and understanding until there were forged structures of thought and speech in terms of which it became understandable and communicable. And so throughout Israel's tradition the Word of God kept pressing for articulation within the corporate medium of covenant reciprocity, creating formal and empirical correlates of its own self-utterance through which it extended its activity in space and time, progressively taking verbal and even written form through the shared understanding and shared response that developed in this people. Thus Israel became in a unique way the bearer of the oracles of God, a church as much as a people charged with priestly and prophetic significance for all mankind and divinely destined for the universalization of its revelatory mission in the advent of God himself in space and time.

By singling out Israel from among the nations for this vicarious service and subjecting it to its long ordeal in history, God adapted Israel to his purpose in such a way as to form within it a womb for the incarnation of his Word and a matrix of appropriate forms of thought and speech for the reception of his revelation in a final and definitive form. And so in the fullness of time Jesus was born of Mary, out of the organic correlation of revelation and response in the life and language of man, to be the Word of God heard and expressed in the truth and grace of perfect human response

to God the Father. In Jesus, God's eternal Word graciously
humbled himself to participate in finite being, submitting to
its limitations and operating within its struggles and structures, thus fulfilling God's revealing and redeeming purpose for his incarnate life as Man on earth and in history.
Such was the life and mission of Jesus Christ the Word made
flesh, who mediated between God and man, reconciling
them in and through himself, and so established a correlation and correspondence between God's self-giving and
man's receiving within which alone God's revelation could
be actualized in man and a true and faithful response could
be yielded by man to God. Thus, in effecting his self-communication to man, the Word of God assimilated the hearing and speaking of man to himself as constitutive ingredients of divine revelation. In him God's articulate
self-utterance became speech to man, through the medium
of human words, and speaks as man to man, for in him God
assumed human speech into union with his own, effecting
it as the human expression of the divine Word.

Jesus Christ himself, then, is the hearing and speaking
man included in the Word of God incarnate, and he is that
in a final and definitive way. In him we do not have to do
simply with the word of God and the response of man,
brought together in some kind of "Nestorian" dualism, but
with the indivisible, all-significant middle term, the divinely
provided response in the vicarious humanity of Jesus Christ.
Once and for all he has become God's exclusive language
to man and he alone must be man's language to God. Here
there operates, as it were, a theological form of Fermat's
principle, in accordance with which the selection of one
among other possible paths in the formulation of natural law
sets the others aside as unentertainable and actually impossible. In himself God is transcendently free and able to create
other possibilities, but the actual incarnation of his eternal
Word once and for all in our contingent existence in Jesus

Christ excludes every other way to the Father and stamps
the vicarious humanity of Christ as the sole norm and law,
as well as the sole ground of acceptable human response to
the Father. Let us note also that in Jesus Christ word and
deed, language and event, were inextricably interwoven in
his revealing and redeeming activity. His words were done
as well as spoken and his deeds spoke as much as his words,
for in him God's Word has become physical, historical
event, while the very fact and existence of Jesus Christ was
and is itself Word of God to mankind. Jesus Christ is the one
place on earth and in history where full reciprocity between
God and man and man and God has been established in such
a way that God's Word and Truth come to us within the
undiminished realities of our spatiotemporal existence and
we human beings may really hear his Word and meet him
face to face. In fact the real text of God's self-revelation to
mankind has once and for all been provided in the humanity
of Jesus Christ, the Word of God personally incarnate in the
flesh.[4]

Here also, however, we have to take fully into account
the fact that the reciprocity established in Jesus Christ is
essentially corporate in nature, so that it could not but effect
a community of reciprocity within which the full movement
of God's incarnate self-revelation and self-communication
would be actualized. Two points of cardinal significance
have to be considered: (*a*) the correlation of the uncreated
Word and Rationality of God and the created word and
rationality of man; and (*b*) the movement from the par-
ticularized form which God's revelation took in the one
Man Jesus to the universalized form which it took through
Pentecost in the apostolic foundation of the church as the
body of Christ.

a. We cannot forget that the Word who became incarnate
in Jesus Christ is the Word through whom all things were
created and in whom they are unceasingly sustained in their

being and rational order. In himself the eternal Word of God is quite independent of what he has made, the free creative source and ground of all finite being. He created the universe out of nothing, gave it a contingent reality and endowed it with a contingent order of its own which he preserves and respects, and remains sovereignly transcendent over it all. In creating the universe he conferred upon it a created rationality different from, yet dependent on, his own uncreated Rationality, and thus gave it an intrinsic lawfulness of its own which is neither self-subsistent nor self-explanatory but which endures before God as the truth and goodness of created reality upheld by his eternal Word. It was into this created rationality (or *logos*) that the Word (or *Logos*) of God entered, assimilating it to himself in the incarnation, in order to become Word of God to man through the medium of human word and rationality and in order to provide from the side of man for an appropriate response in truth and goodness toward God. Created or contingent rationality takes two basic forms, number rationality and word rationality, which we cannot discuss further here.[5] It will be sufficient to note that both these forms of rationality are inextricably intertwined, for neither can come to expression without the other: mathematical representation cannot come to expression without word language, and linguistic representation cannot come to expression without the physical medium to which number rationality is appropriate. Number and word find articulation in coordinated levels of rationality in which each requires the other but in which word is the formal means by which the creation is delivered from being trapped in its mute condition and is made open to what is above and beyond it. In this context the inherent rationality of the contingent universe is found not to be self-contained but to call for a transcendent ground of rationality for its coherent explanation and meaning.

In Jesus Christ, then, the eternal Word of God became man within this world of contingent existence and contingent rationality, sharing to the full the conditions, distinctions, and connections of space and time that characterize the thought and speech of all men, in order to be understandable and communicable as intelligible word to all men. This does not mean that he ceased to be the Word that he is in God; rather, it means that he assimilated human form within the frame of earthly life and action and speech into such oneness with himself as to constitute it not merely the earthen vessel of the Word of God but his actual speaking of it to mankind. That is to say, within the hypostatic union of divine and human nature that took place in Jesus Christ, there is included a union between uncreated and created rationality and between uncreated and created word, so that it is in the rational form of creaturely human word that Jesus Christ mediates God's Word to all mankind.

b. We must now consider more fully how the union of uncreated Word and created word in Jesus Christ makes him not only Word of God to man but also word of man to man, universally communicable within the medium of man's exchange in thought and speech with his fellow man. In order to achieve its end, the self-address of God to man in Jesus Christ had to penetrate, domicile itself, and take form within the interpersonal reciprocities of human society and thereby within the address of man to man. The Word of God which had come "plumb down from above" had to create room for himself and operate within the horizontal dimensions of human existence in order to continue his speaking and acting throughout history. This involved the formation of a nucleus within the speaker-hearer relations of people around Jesus Christ, grounded in the reciprocity between God and man established in him. This then became the controlling basis for the folding out of the self-witness of Christ into witness to Christ informed, empowered, and

used by Christ's self-witness so that it could take the field as
the communicable form of his self-witness in history, i.e., as
the specific form intended by Christ for the proclamation of
God's Word to all men. "That is what took place in the
apostolic foundation of the church and in the apostolic formulation of the kerygma, both as parts of one movement in
which Christ's self-address to man evoked and inspired a
response in word and deed which he assimilated into union
with his own response to God and effected as the authoritative expression of his own kerygma in the world. Thus, in
the apostles as the receiving end of his revealing and reconciling activity, Jesus Christ laid the foundation of the church
which he incorporated into himself as his own body, and
permitted the Word which he put into their mouth to take
the form of proclamation answering to and extending his
own in such a way that it became the controlled unfolding
of his own revelation within the mind and language of the
apostolic foundation. The apostolic proclamation of Christ
was so geared into his self-proclamation that it was used by
him as the shared and corporate medium of understanding
and communication through which he brought his Word in
human and historical form to bear upon mankind throughout the ages. Just as the response of man in Christ was made
a constituent element in the Word of God to man, so the
response of the apostles was assumed by Christ into oneness
with his own to form the means by which the Word of Christ
reached out into history. Thus through the apostolic witness
and proclamation it was Christ himself who was at work
testifying to the mighty acts whereby he had redeemed the
world and offering himself as their Savior and Lord."[6]

It was out of this corporate reciprocity centered in and
creatively controlled by Christ through the outpouring of
his Spirit of Truth upon it that the New Testament Scriptures were born and took shape within the church. They
constitute, therefore, the divinely provided and inspired

linguistic medium which remains of authoritative and critical significance for the whole history of the church of Jesus Christ. Its purpose in this written form in which it has come down to us is to enable us to stand with the original witnesses under the creative impact of the Word which they received and obeyed, and to be drawn into the sphere of its effective operation in the world where we, like them, may learn to repent and believe the gospel, give thanks to God and live in communion with him. Far from obtruding themselves and their own spirituality upon us, the New Testament writers serve the gospel by directing us back to the representative and vicarious humanity of Christ as the creative ground and normative pattern for the actualization of every response to God on our part. It is in fact the humanity of Jesus Christ himself which is the real text underlying the New Testament Scriptures; it is his humanity to which they refer and in terms of which they are to be interpreted.

It must now be noted that with the incarnation of God's Word in Jesus Christ and the community of reciprocity which it created we have a decisively different situation from that which obtained in Old Testament times, for here the forms of thought and speech developed through the historical dialogue of God with Israel are not only fulfilled but transcended and relativized by the final and permanent forms which the Word of God has taken in the life and teaching and saving work of Christ. Here we have to reckon with a profound integration between the Word of God and the word of man which may not be disrupted. The incarnate humanity of the Word, even in his distinctive individuality and physical particularity, is not something that can be discarded like outworn clothing that has served its purpose in the past, for it is constituted the actual form and reality of God's Word addressed to man and is indissolubly bound up with its material content. Hence the basic forms of thought and speech in which the incarnational self-revelation of God

is mediated to us in the New Testament cannot be made the
object of independent investigation in themselves, as if they
could be abstracted from their historical ground and factual
reference in Jesus Christ; nor can they be understood primarily from their place in the social and religious matrix of
Israel or church, as if they could be interpreted merely out
of the subjective states of those who received God's revelation; they can only be understood from their place in the
normative and definitive structure of the Word made flesh
in his solidarity with human and physical being in space and
time.

We come back to the point, then, that it is a Bible-related
revelation of God that we have in view and seek to interpret
in Christian theology, for it is in this articulate form of
human word, spoken and written, which the Word of God
has taken in space and time, that God continues to make
himself known to us. It must be noted, however, that the
relation between God's self-revelation and the Holy Scriptures in and through which it is mediated is essentially asymmetric. In a profound sense this is even true of the relation
between the Word of God and the word of man in Jesus
Christ himself, for he is word of man in answer to God only
in that he is first and foremost Word of God become man.
This is why the New Testament insists so strongly and con-
sistently on the obedience of the incarnate Son to God the
Father. Of course in Jesus Christ himself, as we have noted,
there is a hypostatic union of divine and human word in his
one Person. Therefore in him we have to reckon with a
first-order relation ontologically inseparable from the fact
that the Word *became* man, a relation such that the human
word *is* Word of God. But in the relation between divine
revelation and the language of the Holy Scriptures we have
only a second-order relation in which the human word of
the Scripture is not ontologically identical with the incarnate
Word. Since this second-order relation is contingent upon

and controlled by the first-order relation of hypostatic union in Christ himself, we may well hold that here also, although on a different level of reality, we have a relation between the divine and the human factors in which they may neither be divided from nor confused with each other. In this case the relation of asymmetry is very different, for it obtains in a relation not of ontological identity but of ontological difference. The Holy Scripture *is* not Jesus Christ, the Word of God incarnate. We may express this differently by saying that Jesus Christ the incarnate Word of God is not merely a reflection of divine Light, a transparent medium through which that Light shines into the world, nor is he therefore merely a witness to the Light, for he is identical with the Light to which he bears witness. He is in fact "the real Light," the Reality of the enlightening Light of God of which all created light is a reflection and to which it bears witness (John 1:9). In the same way we must say that the Holy Scriptures are not themselves the real Light that Christ is, but are what they are only as enlightened by him and as they therefore bear witness to him beyond themselves. In no way can the light of the Scriptures substitute for the Light of Christ, for they are entirely subordinate to his Light and are themselves light only as they are lit by his Light. Indeed it may be said that if the Scriptures are treated as having a light inherent in themselves, they are deprived of their true light which they have by reflecting the Light of Christ beyond themselves—and then the light that is in them is turned into a kind of darkness.

The Scriptures of the Old and New Testaments rightly evoke from us profound respect and veneration not because of what they are in themselves but because of the divine revelation mediated in and through them. That is why we speak of them as "Holy" Scriptures.[7] Since God's self-revelation in and through the Bible must be experienced and cognized in the reality it is apart from the words and statements of the Bible, something would appear to have gone wrong if we become too obsessed with the Bible, as so often happens in the stress that is laid upon its inspiration when our attention is directed to the Bible itself instead of to what it is intended to bear witness. It must be granted that we understand the Bible properly when we attend jointly to the text and the divine realities to which it directs us, yet only in such a way that our attention to the text is subordinated to the realities beyond it. So soon as we switch the focus of our attention from those realities to the text itself, the text tends to lose its in-depth significance.[8]

This is entirely consistent with the realist relation between sign or word and reality signified or indicated, which we discussed earlier. Signs or words fulfill their semantic function properly when we attend away from them to the realities they signify or intend. Through their correlation with those realities they cease to be objects of attention in themselves but serve as transparent media through which those realities show themselves. They are to be understood, therefore, as signs or words through their function in directing our attention away from themselves, and they become obscure or lose their proper meaning when they are allowed to obtrude themselves on us as the immediate objects of our attention. Transferring this to the Bible, we may say that we rely upon the Bible for its guidance in directing our understanding to the Word of God which sounds through it, or the Truth of God which shines through it. In the fulfillment of that semantic service the Bible effaces itself before the immediacy and compulsion of God's self-revelation, which we experience, certainly through the Bible, but in its own divine reality which is independent of the Bible. There is indeed, then, a two-way relation between divine revelation and the Bible, but it is an asymmetrical relation in which ontological priority and authoritative primacy must be given to divine revelation and not to the Bible. It is the

subordination of the Bible to that revelation and the semantic service it fulfills in mediating that revelation to us that
give the Bible its singular status in our respect and its decisive authority in our knowledge of God.

So far we have been treating the Bible in the belief that
it really is the product of God's self-revealing to mankind
and must be understood in its continuing correlation with
activity on God's part. This is all-important, for if we do not
believe this to be the case, our attitude to the Bible and our
interpretation of it are bound to be very different from what
they will be if we do believe it.[9] Something quite ultimate
is at stake here. Now, whatever we may believe about it, the
Bible certainly claims to speak of a living God who interacts
with what he has made, and whose self-revelation to man in
history has reached its decisive point in the incarnation of
God's Word in Jesus Christ. People may well reject that
claim, but it does not entitle them to approach the Bible as
if it did not mean to speak of such a God, or therefore to
interpret its language and statements, its witness, proclamation, and teaching, as if they were not intentionally directed
to the activity of such a living, speaking God.

Given, then, a *bona fide* approach to the Holy Scriptures
in which we seek, at least initially, to understand them in
accordance with their own intentions and claims, a fundamental question must be raised before serious interpretation begins. Do we in fact operate with a framework of
thought which will not allow us to believe in such a God,
a God who creatively interacts with our world and makes
himself known within space and time? If we do operate with
such an antecedent framework of thought, what is the underlying outlook that gives it its power over us? Is it some
kind of epistemological and cosmological dualism that dis-
rupts the ontological integration between form and subject
matter and thereby affects all our regulative convictions and
even shapes the end results of our exegesis and interpreta-

tion of the biblical documents? In this event we would take up a "disinterested" attitude in our inquiry, and set about the task of interpretation by working with forms of thought and patterns of speech detached from and uncontrolled by the subject matter, forms and patterns which are open to any meaning which we may consciously or unconsciously give them, and which we can freely deploy as an interpretative instrument in order to make the biblical subject matter understandable to ourselves in our own cultural situation. But then we would be trapped in the arbitrary procedures and disastrous mistakes which realist scientific knowledge in its own sphere has exposed and from which it has turned away. On the other hand, if we reject an approach of this kind and the damaging dualisms that govern it, and if we adopt another outlook in accordance with which form and subject matter are never separated but are recognized always to inhere in one another both in reality itself at all levels and in our knowledge of it, how are we to treat the Bible with a view to interpreting and understanding its message? In this event we must try to allow the Bible to interpret itself to us out of the inherence of form and subject matter already latent in it, and therefore out of its own inherent significance. We must seek to understand the Bible out of the intelligible forms intrinsically embodied in its actual subject matter, and therefore in the semantic correlation of what it says and that to which it refers.[10]

Behind all this, however, we have to reckon with the truth of what the Bible talks about, namely, a living God who creatively interacts with man in the world and makes himself known to him in a controlling, articulate, and informing way; that is, we have to reckon with the reality of God's self-revelation to mankind in and through the Holy Scriptures. In addition to the initial commitment which in good faith we must surely make to what the Bible intends to say, if we are not to prejudge its message from the very start, another commitment is laid upon us by the reality of the self-revealing God to which the Bible claims to refer beyond itself. This is not a commitment which we may avoid if we are to engage in serious in-depth interpretation of the Bible in its correlation with God's self-revelation, for otherwise we would artificially restrict our interpretation merely to the surface level of biblical statements and narratives without giving any attention to their objective reference. A realist interpretation of the Bible in its intimate correlation with God's self-revelation will involve a cross-level movement of thought in which we seek to understand the text and its message at the same time. We rely on what the Bible says as a guide to our understanding of what it talks about, and in the light of what it talks about we clarify our understanding of what it says, although, of course, ontological priority must be accorded to what the Bible talks about or to the realities to which it refers.

We are now in a position to assert that a realist interpretation of the Holy Scriptures involves at once a theologico-scientific commitment to the reality and intelligibility of what they talk about and a theologico-scientific handling of the objective reference of what they have to say.

While this commitment to the truth of the biblical message, or rather to the truth of God's self-revelation mediated through the Bible, is an intensely personal act of trust in which our whole being is implicated, it is nevertheless a commitment which is objectively and not subjectively grounded and controlled.[11] It is the freely evoked, empirical submission of our minds to the self-evidencing Reality of God, which bears upon us as we listen to the message of the Bible, and which lays upon us an obligation to recognize, reverence, and assent to it that we may not rationally or in good conscience resist. This external or objective anchoring of our commitment saves that commitment from being subjective or arbitrary, for it binds our faith and understanding to what exists independently of our knowing of it and is universally real and true, and it thereby stakes out the ground for a rigorously scientific approach to interpretation. At the same time, the objective reference of commitment reinforces a proper scientific handling of biblical language and statements in the light of the objective or ontological references they promote, and not in the light of the subjective attitudes and emotions which they may express or arouse.[12] In direct referential relations of this kind questions of truth and falsity are raised, which does not happen when biblical language and statements are interpreted indirectly, obliquely, or metaphorically. In this case the semantic bearing of the references upon the reality they intend must be tested, but only in the light of that reality; for that reality alone, and not our subjective reactions, must be the judge of their truth or falsity. By the very nature of their objective reference biblical reports point us beyond themselves altogether, and thereby judge themselves as falling short of their objective, but since they refer to objective relations and intelligibilities in the events and realities to which they bear witness, the adequacy of their references must be examined in the light of those relations and intelligibilities. This is not something that can be carried out in any impersonal way or by applying some formal methodological test; it can only be done by a person or rational agent exercising a trained spiritual and theological judgment. It is this combination of the personal and the objective which is highly distinctive of theologico-scientific activity in biblical interpretation.

In view of the foregoing discussion of the asymmetric correlation between God's self-revelation and the Holy Scriptures which continue to mediate that revelation in history, what *general guidelines* may be offered for the actual task of biblical interpretation? If we are to take our cue from Athanasius, and the kind of hermeneutical activity that preceded and underlay the classical conciliar theology, to which all Christendom is so heavily indebted, three or four such guidelines may be considered.[13] If interpretation is to be faithful to what the Bible discloses itself to be, it must operate within the boundaries of the ways and acts of God out of which the various Scriptures arose. Hence it must (1) attend to the "scope" of divine revelation in the Scriptures, (2) respect the objective grounding and ordering of Scriptural statements in the "economic" reality of the Words and Acts of God himself, (3) be guided by an interpretative framework of thought derived from the connections and coherences in the biblical subject matter, and (4) clarify and check interpretations in accordance with "the canon of truth." Clearly all of these overlap with one another.

1. THE SCOPE OF THE BIBLE

In one of his early essays Karl Barth wrote about "the strange new world within the Bible," by which he meant the world of divine Reality which breaks into ours and opens its range far beyond itself by giving our world an objective and a perspective centered in God himself.[14] It is only by entering this strange new world that we can come to grips with the contents of the Bible, and that means that we must learn to entrust our thought and our destiny to it and let it carry us far beyond ourselves, disturbing though that may be. This is very close to what the Greek fathers meant by the *scope* of the Holy Scriptures, the whole new world of meaning centered in God, and in his Words and Works, which we cannot understand from a center in ourselves. It is only within this new divine perspective and in accordance with the distinctive slant it imposes upon the Scriptures that they may be faithfully interpreted and properly understood. In the language which we have been using, the scope of the Bible relates to the objective reference of its component Scriptures, which gives them their line of direction and their ultimate coherence, and at the same time determines the way in which they are to be treated. Thus the word "scope" can be used in a wide sense to describe the general perspective or frame of reference within which the Scriptures are rightly to be interpreted, and in a deeper sense to denote the basic pattern of meaning that is discerned when the interpreter not only looks at the written words or statements but looks through them at the objective center of reference beyond.

The question must be raised as to how we get inside this new world of meaning or come to share in the new perspective, especially if it is so radically new that we could have no inkling of it beforehand. That was a question constantly posed to the early church on the boundaries between Christian and Hellenic thought. The answer given, for example by Clement of Alexandria, was that here we have to reckon with realities which, like the first principles in geometry or the simple facts of perception, are known on the strength not of anything else but of themselves, that is, through a basic act of assent or faith in recognition of and in response to those realities.[15] The right way to break through into the new realm of meaning or truth, therefore, is the way of faith, for unless we believe we will not understand.[16] Now faith involves a conceptual assent to the unseen reality, for the proof of an unknown reality is its own evidence and the evident assent it calls forth from us. That is to say, if we are really to understand, we must willingly allow our minds to fall under the compulsive self-evidence of the reality, otherwise we merely lapse back uncritically into our own false preconceptions. What is needed is an anticipatory or proleptic conception derived from initial contact with the hitherto unknown reality, for without a basic clue of this kind we will never learn anything new.[17]

This is certainly not easy with the "strange new world" which meets us in the Bible, for we are unable to grasp or conceptualize it in terms of what we have experienced elsewhere or already know, and for it we need quite new ways of thinking and understanding. This is possible only if we persistently attend to the organization of conceptual form and material content already embodied in what the Bible says, let it talk to us, and allow ourselves to be directed by the semantic bearing of what it says upon the objective events and realities it intends, so that our minds may fall under the power of their inherent intelligibility or *logos*. This is a difficulty that crops up again and again for those who already operate within the scope of the Holy Scriptures, when they are presented with novelties in the text and in the subject matter alike, of which they are unable to make rational sense in terms of any normal framework of thought. Instead of dismissing them right away as quite unintelligible, however, as doubtless they may be tempted to do, they must rather try to understand them, if possible and as far as possible, out of a conjoint signification of their own in which the meaning of the realities denoted and the meaning of the terms denoting them are grasped at the same time and are matched to each other.[18] This will entail a modification or a reconstruction of what they already claim to know and accept as rational or significant. A repentant rethinking of this kind is steadily called for when we seek to interpret the message of the Holy Scripture out of its own strange perspective and out of its own inherent demands and semantic reference. The Greek fathers were surely right when they insisted that in a genuine act of knowledge we seek to apprehend something new or hitherto unknown or unique by allowing it in its own reality to prove itself to us and disclose its intrinsic significance and truth, and thus to impress on our minds the appropriate way in which it is to be understood and expressed.

It must be pointed out that this way of entering into the new world of meaning and of learning how to interpret the

Bible within its own scope of significance is essentially an epistemic and not a psychological operation.[19] What is involved, then, is a subject/object and not a subject/subject relation. Interpretation operates on two levels, for there is a subject/object relation between the interpreter and the text, and within the text there is a subject/object relation between the biblical writer and what he intends to signify, or between the biblical witness and that to which he bears witness. Everything goes wrong if the interpreter attempts to transcend the subject/object relation by trying to relate his own subject directly to the subject of the biblical witness (the individual or the community), in which he can only begin with his own self-understanding and end with his self-understanding under the delusion that he can understand the author better than he can understand himself. It goes entirely wrong, for it destroys the whole scope or objective frame of reference within which the Bible presents and interprets itself to us. In the next section we shall reckon with the fact that here in biblical interpretation as in theological activity we must be concerned to penetrate into what we have called object/object relations, that is, the relations inherent in the objective realities which control our subject/object relations and prevent them from lapsing into subjective or psychologizing movements of thought in which we would inevitably be trapped within the circle of our self-centered preconceptions and private opinions.

To seek an understanding interpretation of biblical documents, then, does not mean that we try to divine the subjective reactions and states of their authors, but rather that we respond to their call to share with them the same objective orientation toward the living, speaking, and acting God as they have found themselves obliged to adopt—often, quite obviously, against the grain of their own desires and in conflict with their prejudgments. Hence as we attend to what they actually say as carefully as we can, we try to follow through the semantic reference of their witness and reports so that we also may experience and apprehend the living God in the Reality of his own Words and Acts for ourselves. As we do that we find ourselves confronted with the ultimate realities of God's self-revelation and self-communication. These realities stake out for us the ground on which alone they may be known and understood, and thereby they constitute the scope or perspective within which all witness and reports on the part of the biblical authors are to be interpreted. Thus, so far as the New Testament Scriptures are concerned, the incarnation and resurrection of Jesus Christ constituted the ground on which they were understood and validated, brought about a radically new conception of God and a complete transformation of man's outlook in terms of a new divine order, and—thus bracketing within them the whole life, activity, and passion of Jesus Christ— gave rise to the basic framework within which the New Testament Scriptures are set and have to be interpreted.[20] That is to say, the incarnation, passion, and resurrection of Jesus Christ gave the New Testament the comprehensive scope within which all its writings took shape and form. Thus these realities forced themselves upon the mind of the Christian community in sharp antithesis to what people had believed about God and in genuine conflict with the framework of secular thought or the prevailing world view; they took root in the church, which they had called into existence, only through a seismic restructuring of people's religious and intellectual beliefs. Through the New Testament Scriptures the self-revelation and self-communication of God in the incarnation, passion, and resurrection of Jesus Christ continue to supply the objective framework within which the gospel is to be understood and the Scriptures are to be interpreted. But they are ultimates, carrying their own authority and calling for the intelligent commitment of faith, and they provide the irreducible ground upon which continuing theologico-scientific inquiry and formulation take place.

A great deal has been made in modern biblical scholarship of what is called the "pluralism" manifest in the New Testament writings, and that is understandable once they are subjected to critical analysis apart from the basic framework of the New Testament in which they are set. But a very different picture emerges when we attend to the actual scope within which they have arisen and taken shape. Then for all their rich diversity they are found to have a deep underlying unity in Jesus Christ the incarnate and risen Lord, who is the dynamic center and the objective focus of their creative integration. But that calls for a way of interpretation in which the images or patterns at the linguistic and theological levels are stereoscopically coordinated in our viewing, for it is through the scope of their conjoint reference that real meaning and coherence come to light.

The interpreter operates, therefore, on both levels at the same time. At the level of the text the interpreter seeks to keep to what Athanasius called "the scope and character of Holy Scripture." By that he meant not only the peculiarities of linguistic expression and syntactic structure which may have arisen under the impact of divine revelation, but the customary way in which the Scriptures take language developed to describe our experience in this world and give it a new sense beyond commonly accepted usage to convey its message about God and man. It is, then, in accordance with this new slant or shift in meaning that the sense of a particular passage is to be judged, that is, within the general direction and coherent tenor of biblical usage. The interpreter must operate at a deeper level than this, however, by keeping to what Athanasius called "the scope of faith." By that he meant the objective meaning that lies behind the written words, arising out of the ontological orientation constituted by what the Scriptures tell us of the ways and works of God and in accordance with the religious experience which they evoke. That is to say, interpretation of biblical statements and reports must reflect "the mind" of the Holy Scriptures, or more specifically "the Mind of Christ," which has left its imprint upon them. Strictly speaking, Christ himself is the scope of the Scriptures, so that it is only through focusing constantly upon him, dwelling in his Word and assimilating his Mind, that the interpreter can discern the real meaning of the Scriptures. What is required, then, is a theological interpretation of the Scriptures under the direction of their ostensive reference to God's self-revelation in Jesus Christ and within the general perspective of faith.

2. THE "ECONOMIC" GROUND AND STRUCTURE OF BIBLICAL STATEMENTS

We have just been considering the point that the Holy Scriptures are rightly interpreted within the general orientation of meaning set up by their subject matter, the new dimension of God's self-revelation which gave them their distinctive perspective and character. This is a way of interpreting biblical statements and reports in accordance with the objective pole of their reference. We must now give attention to the point that the subject/object relationship which this involves requires to be grounded in and controlled by what we have earlier spoken of as "object/object" relations, that is, intelligible relations inherent in the objective realities to which the Holy Scriptures bear witness. Since they point beyond themselves to these given realities, biblical statements manifest among themselves a coherent pattern of reference determined by their common point of reference. But we have to reckon with something more than this, namely, with the fact that biblical statements are so grounded in and controlled by a basic pattern of truth in those objective realities that it is imprinted upon them. Thus the distinctive kind of order which informs and gives coherence to biblical statements is not one which they have independently in themselves which can be read off their grammatical, syntactic, or formal-logical sequence, but one which they acquire from beyond themselves as through the mighty *canto fermo* of his Word God calls them into contrapuntal relation, as it were, to the ordered pattern of events in his saving and revealing self-communication to mankind through Israel and in Jesus Christ. This is the intelligible order disclosed in what the Greek fathers called the "economic condescension" of God in the incarnation of his Son and Word in Jesus Christ, or in his "human economy" toward us.[21]

In the New Testament and early Christian writings the term "economy" was used to speak of the orderly line of action God has taken in the fulfillment of his saving purpose for mankind, i.e., the dispensation of his grace which has taken the form of the self-humbling of God the Son in the incarnation and Passion of Jesus Christ. Our concern at the moment is with the profound epistemological implications of this "economic condescension" which patristic theology was not slow to draw out for biblical interpretation and theological statement. Just as we think of the incarnation as God becoming man in order to become one with man and thereby to redeem man from within the depths of his human nature, so we may think of the incarnation as God the Word becoming man in order to adapt himself to man in his weakness and lack of ability and to assimilate human modes of thought and speech to himself, and thereby to effect real communication between God and man and man and God. Granted, then, that human modes of thought and speech are utterly inadequate to speak of God or to convey divine Truth, nevertheless as they have been assumed, transformed, and used in God's self-revelation they are made to indicate more than they can express and to convey divine Truth beyond their natural capacity. It was in the light of this "economic condescension" of God in which he accommodates his self-revelation to man that the fathers regarded the Old Testament Scriptures as registering the gradual self-revelation of God to his people in anticipation of the incarnational fullness and finality of his self-communication to mankind in Jesus Christ.[22] When in him the Word actually became flesh, God forged the distinctive language whereby he forever speaks to man and man may speak to God and of God. And since it was through the specific forms of thought and speech which God sanctified and adapted to his self-revelation in Jesus Christ that the New Testament Scriptures took shape, it is surely as such that they should be appreciated and interpreted, i.e., in accordance with the "human economy" of God's Word.[23] Although these human forms of thought and speech found in the Scriptures are unable of themselves to convey the Word of God, they are nevertheless grounded and structured through the incarnation in the very Logos who inheres eternally in the Being of God and are the vehicles of his address to mankind. Hence if we are properly to interpret and understand biblical statements, we must learn to trace back their objective reference beyond what is written to their source in the infinite depth of Truth in the Being of God, and if we are to do that we must follow the economic line of divine action that gave rise to them in space and time and continues to govern their meaning.

Quite evidently, everything depends on whether we understand the "economic condescension" of God in the incarnation in a realist way or not, i.e., whether we believe that in Jesus Christ we are in direct contact with the ultimate Reality and Truth of God in our spatiotemporal existence or not.[24] If this were not the case, we could not reckon on any objective connection between what the New Testament tells us about God and what God is in himself independently of the New Testament. And in that event we would have

no ground for claiming that the human forms of thought
and speech employed in the Scriptures are harnessed to
God's creative self-revelation in such a way that they are
enabled to direct us ostensively to divine realities and relations utterly beyond themselves. We could only interpret
them primarily in accordance with what they are as *human*
forms of thought and speech, that is, with only a this-worldly
creaturely meaning and with, at most, a merely symbolic,
mythological, or oblique reference to God. If we do not
understand the "economic condescension" realistically,
then the term "economy" will be taken to indicate that we
can speak of God's incarnate self-humbling and self-revelation only by way of "reserve," which is tantamount to as-
serting that God cannot be taken really to be in himself what
he appears to us to be in his manifestation in Jesus Christ
toward us.

What is at stake here is the question whether biblical
statements about God—for example, about his Fatherhood
in respect to Jesus Christ his incarnate Son—are related to
what they claim to signify merely in a conventional way
(thesei) or in a real way *(physei)*. [25] Only if God really became
man in Jesus Christ, and really made our human nature his
own in him, may we say that statements of this kind are
related to what God is in himself in a real and not in a
merely conventional or fictional way, for then they are
economically grounded and structured in God's own acts of
self-revelation and self-communication and are governed by
them. But if the incarnation and the economy are not taken
seriously, as the New Testament witness certainly means
them to be, then such statements have no relation to reality
in God but only the significance we may want to put into
them in accordance with our own presuppositions or conve-
nience, but of course in this case we would have no criterion
to judge between statement and statement or truth and

falsity, and we would be lost in the morass of mythology and allegory.

This is precisely the problem that faced the fathers of the church at the Council of Nicaea, when they found themselves forced to come to a more precise understanding of what it meant to say about Jesus Christ that he is *of* God, for as they realized it is upon the answer to that question that the whole evangelical interpretation of the New Testament, and indeed of the Bible, depends. In what sense is Jesus Christ *Son* of God the *Father?* The terms "son" and "father" carry a creaturely content with which we are familiar in the interrelations between a human father and a human son, and as such they may not be read back into the inner relations of God's own Being. Are the images of sonship and fatherhood, then, no more than empty names conventionally related to God as detachable, imaginary imitations of divine Reality and therefore quite changeable and relative with no permanent value? Or are they terms which, inadequate as they are in themselves, point ostensively to real relations in God beyond themselves, since they are economically rooted in God's own *self-*giving and *self-*revealing in Jesus Christ and are therefore ultimately real and valid in God as well as for us? As they sifted through the New Testament Scriptures, those who met at Nicaea were convinced that the relation of the Father to the Son and of the Son to the Father constitutes the basic ontological relationship or reciprocity in the Godhead in which all the language of the gospel is finally rooted and shaped. "All things have been delivered unto me of my Father: and no one knows who the Son is, save the Father; and who the Father is, save the Son, and he to whom the Son wills to reveal him"[26] (Luke 10:22; Matt. 11:27). That is to say, a mutual relation of knowing and being obtains between the Father and the Son in the Godhead, and it is as that relation

is actualized through the incarnation between Jesus Christ
and God the Father that it becomes possible for us to know
God in and through Jesus Christ in such a way that our
knowledge terminates on the ultimate Reality of God himself.

In this context the Nicene fathers set about examining
and testing the various expressions, images, and representations used of God in the New Testament, correlating them
with the objective realities and relations they were taken to
serve, in order to allow the human forms of thought and
speech which we have to use to be modified and corrected
by relation to one another within their common frame of
reference, i.e., within the scope set by Christ himself and his
relation as incarnate Son to the Father. Through hard exegetical and critical activity of this kind they came up with
the concept of the consubstantial relation of the incarnate
Son to the Father, which they adopted in order to cut
through the self-contradictions and confusions that had
arisen in the church through forced interpretations of biblical language and the misuse of biblical images, and in order
thereby to lay bare the central nerve of the evangelical and
apostolic message in the directness and simplicity of the
relation of Jesus Christ to God the Father. The *homoousion,*
the insight that Jesus Christ the incarnate Son is "of one and
the same being with God the Father," God of God and
Light of Light, is thus a supreme example of strict theological understanding arising out of the interpretation of biblical statements, derived by following the ostensive reference
of biblical images and representations, and by giving com-
pressed expression in exact and equivalent language, not so
much to the biblical terms themselves but to the objective
meaning or reality they were designed to point out and
convey. Once established, however, the *homoousion* served
as a further guide to the interpretation of the Holy Scriptures, although of course it continued to be subordinate to

and revisable in the light of the self-revelation of God as mediated through the apostolic witness embodied in the New Testament. The *homoousion,* therefore, is not a speculative construction, an attempt to break through to the reality of God by the power of human thought, or an interpretation extrinsically imposed upon the evangelical tradition by the theologians of the church. Rather is it a truth which forced itself upon the understanding of the church as it allowed the biblical witness to imprint its own conceptual pattern upon its mind.[27] In and through its formulation, the inner logic of grace in the economic condescension of God in Jesus Christ and the inherent intelligibility of divine Reality in the immanent relations within the Godhead came to expression in a disciplined theological way. Therein an irreversible step in the understanding of the church was taken which has had a decisive impact on subsequent interpretation of the Holy Scriptures and the formulation of Christian doctrine. The history of the church and its handling of the Bible shows that a realist interpretation of God's self-revelation in and through the Bible requires a realist understanding of the incarnation and the economic grounding and structuring of biblical forms of thought and speech in God himself.

3. An Interpretative Framework of Thought

In all coherent rational discourse or writing, statements have a twofold reference: a primary reference which is denotative or semantic, and a secondary reference which is connotative or syntactic. Strictly speaking neither functions meaningfully without the other, for the former without the latter would be blind, and the latter without the former would be empty. This is very evident in our handling of propositions in natural science—especially in the realist orientation of science, which rejects the separation of form and being. It is evident in the interrelation between what Einstein called the "objective or intuitive" reference and the "logical-formal" reference. This applies no less to biblical and theological statements, as I have shown at length elsewhere.[28] In discussing the scope of the Bible and the economic ground and structure of biblical statements, we have been mainly concerned with their objective or semantic reference, but now we must give attention to the all-important point that the functioning of that reference relies upon the coherence of biblical statements with each other. It is in virtue of the hinge between syntactic and semantic relations that biblical statements bear effectively on their objective pole, but it is in virtue of the coherent pattern of thought which those statements comprise that they may serve the disclosure of a coherent pattern of intelligibility in the object to which they direct us. Just as words bear significantly upon their object, not in isolation from one another but only in the context of sentences, so statements bear significantly upon an intelligible pattern of truth in their objective pole when they are structured together into a coherent pattern of reference. This is partly why we have already devoted so much attention to the general scope or coherent perspective of the Bible and to the economic grounding and structuring of biblical concepts in God's self-revelation which gives an objective pattern to the whole semantic focus of the biblical message.

In view of the way in which the primary reference of biblical statements to God relies upon the secondary reference of those statements to one another in coherent sequences, a great deal of attention must also be given to how the statements in biblical texts are to be read within their own syntactical or formal-logical structures and within the whole context in which they are found. This must be done if reasonable interpretation is to be offered and any rational account of the meaning to be assigned to them is to be given. In fact, only if we pay careful attention to the orderly connections built up by words, sentences, and continuous reports may we be in a position to discern how, through their objective reference, the Holy Scriptures may yield their own interpretation. Moreover, it is when we allow the biblical texts to declare their own syntactical meaning to us in this way that we are restrained from imposing upon them an objective meaning alien to what they actually say.

Determination of the coherent patterns of sense and meaning in biblical passages and documents is not so easy as it might at first appear on the syntactic and semantic surface. Much hard thought and work is required in exegetical and critical inquiry to lay bare what we call their inner rational sequence. The interpreter must seek to clarify rather more than the grammatico-syntactical sense of passages. He must probe into the reasonable ground underlying their linguistic signification, and that needs a comparative examination of their signifying components including the many images, analogies, figures, representations, and idioms that are employed, in order to determine as far as possible their exact sense and then to distill out of them and bring to consistent expression the basic conceptuality they carry. Analytical and synthetical work of this kind calls for a keen perception and judgment on the part of the interpreter in deciding what is finally irrelevant overtone and what is essential to the real meaning intended. It is only as the linguistic and conceptual forms are matched to one another that the inner rational sequence may be disclosed in an adequate and semantically helpful way.

On the other hand, we must be on our guard against concentrating so much on grammatico-syntactical and formal-logical sequences and structures that we force biblical statements into a closed coherence which cuts short their objective reference, for then they become finally empty of meaning. The sequence or coherence which biblical statements have with one another is rather more than a grammatico-syntactic or logico-formal one, for it derives ultimately from the subject matter itself. And, as we have seen, this means not merely that the coherent pattern they manifest is due to a common point of reference beyond themselves, but that it reflects and is controlled by an intrinsic pattern of coherence in that common object of reference. Hence we must take great care to preserve the open texture of the inner rational sequence of biblical statements, in virtue of which the intrinsic intelligibility of its objective pole may shine through to us, if we are really to understand and express that inner rational sequence in a consistent way. This is a very significant discovery about all formal-logical and formal-syntactic systems that modern mathematics has brought home to us with great force, namely, that no such system (provided it is rich enough) can be complete and consistent at the same time—otherwise it is no more than a meaningless game.[29] If it is to be consistent and meaningful, it must be incomplete, for its internal consistency depends on reference to a higher level of coherent significance beyond itself. This was in fact a point made long ago by Duns Scotus when he insisted that in any complex of secondary "intentions" there must be at least one or two primary "intentions," otherwise the complex lacks real meaning.[30] Translated into our concern here, this means that we are unable even to determine the formal-syntactic coherence of biblical statements or passages in any consistent way unless we introduce into the equation at least some *direct references* to objective realities and intelligibilities beyond the statements themselves, for it is finally through that metasyntactic reference that syntactic systems may be coherently organized. In words that we have used earlier, no syntactics contains its own semantics. When interpretation is prepared to give a pivotal place in the determination of a consistent and coherent connection in biblical statements to their objective semantic reference, many of the difficulties and perplexities that crop up on the linguistic level disappear, and reasonable and legitimate interpretation of biblical passages results, without distortion or violence and certainly without the need to impose oblique or mythological "meanings" which have no backing in objective reality.

It should now be clear that if we are to reach an adequate and consistent understanding of biblical texts and passages even at their linguistic and syntactic level, we must be prepared to offer a theological interpretation of them by subjecting the language used to the realities it signifies and attend to the bearing of its coherent patterns upon the self-revelation of God which it manifestly intends. The sequences and coherences on the linguistic and syntactic level will then be interpreted as counter themes called forth and organized at their boundary conditions by the creative impact of the Word of God. It is in the semantic relation between the human word and the divine Word that the basic clues to understanding will be found, for the higher level of God's Word comprehends the operation of the human word at the lower level and forms its meaningful reference to itself. That is the point where theological interpretation must start, where the linguistic and theological forms are matched to one another in such a way that through their conjunction we are able to gain our anticipatory glimpses or conceptions of objective patterns of truth. With their help we then go on to develop an initial interpretative framework of theological concepts which we may use as a guide to further interpretation of the Holy Scriptures but which will be progressively revised and deepened in the course of that interpretative activity. It is a framework, of course, which will be organized not logically, but contrapuntally, and which will function as a transparent medium or a "disclosure model" through which we allow our understanding more and more to yield obediently to the self-revelation of God himself. The patristic concepts of a "consubstantial relation" or a "hypostatic union" between

the incarnate Son and God the Father may properly be
regarded as disclosure models in this sense, for they serve
as conceptual lenses or as interpretative instruments for ev-
er-deepening and ever-widening understanding of God's
self-revelation in Jesus Christ, in the course of which they
themselves are or ought to be continuously revised and
refined in the light of what becomes disclosed to us through
them. Provisional, revisable interpretative frameworks of
this kind are essential for genuine theological interpretation
of the Holy Scriptures, but they must never be allowed to
get out of hand in such a way that they force us to trim the
realities signified by the Holy Scriptures in order to make
them fit in with a sense we may want to put upon them.

It must be emphasized, then, that true and faithful interpretation of the Bible involves the construction of a consistent line of theological statements through which the "inner
logic" of the biblical message becomes disclosed. Then interpretation must build on that foundation, using what has
already been done accurately and carefully as its guide in
deepening understanding of the Scriptures. If interpretation
really is in touch with the Truth of God's self-revelation, it
will be harnessed to the operation of that Truth in and
through the Scriptures and will advance along with it to the
end toward which it leads us. Not to advance in this way
would be a sign that interpretation is not really in touch with
the objective realities of God or in line with the basic conceptual patterns they have imprinted upon the Scriptures.
The interpretative framework of theological thought that is
generated in this way serves the Bible as a medium through
which it may continue to reflect its meaning and reflect it
ever more profoundly.

4. THE CANON OF TRUTH

Appeal to "the canon of truth" is the last of the general
guidelines which we have taken from the exegetical and

interpretative work that underlay the formulation of basic theological doctrine in the Nicene era of the church. When all is said and done in biblical interpretation and theological formulation, the ultimate criterion to which appeal is to be made is the Truth itself, that Truth independent of themselves to which the Holy Scriptures direct us and to which they themselves are subject. All faithful interpretation must allow the Truth to assert itself in its own intrinsic weight and majesty and to maintain its own ground over against us and our prejudices, for in the last resort we have to reckon with the fact that God alone can name himself and bear witness to himself and thus prove himself to us.[31]

This means that our interpretation and understanding of the Bible cannot be established or defended simply by appealing to biblical texts or passages or even biblical concepts, but only through listening to the truths they signify or attest and allowing our minds to be objectively determined by them. That is to say, biblical statements are to be treated, not as containing or embodying the Truth of God in themselves, but as pointing, under the leading of the Spirit of Truth, to Jesus Christ himself who is the Truth. We have to recognize the fact, therefore, that the Scriptures indicate much more than can be expressed, and that there is much more to their truth than can be reduced to words. We could not know the Truth of God had he not condescended in Jesus Christ to be one with us in our human nature, and thus to present himself to us within the lowliness of our creaturely capacity and at the same time to lift us up in Jesus Christ to know him in some measure as he is in himself. However, even when we do apprehend the Truth of God in this way, we are quite unable to comprehend him, for he infinitely transcends all our human conceptions of him.[32]

The implication of this is that we may know God and interpret his self-revelation only in the attitude and context of worship and within the fellowship of the church, where to the godly reason God is more to be adored than expressed. It is only as we allow ourselves, within the fellowship of faith and through constant meditation on the Holy Scriptures, to come under the creative impact of God's self-revelation that we may acquire the disciplined spiritual perception or insight which enables us to discriminate between our conceptions of the Truth and the Truth itself. This is not a gift which we can acquire and operate for ourselves alone but one which we may have only as we share it with others in common listening to God's Word and in common adoration and worship of God through the Son and in the one Spirit. Discriminating discernment mediated to us in this way is properly the obedient readiness on our part to submit to the Truth in God as the ultimate Judge of the rightness or wrongness of our interpretations or the truth or falsity of our understanding of his self-revelation.

That is surely the primary sense in which we may take appeal to the canon of truth as a constant guide in biblical interpretation and understanding, but there is also a secondary sense which we must note. This is more apparent in one of the Latin equivalents, *regula fidei,* where the center of gravity is shifted from the truth itself to a set of basic truths or canonical doctrines of the faith which become the authoritative criteria with reference to which interpretation may be judged right or wrong, true or false.[33] In actual practice, appeal was made in this way to the Apostles' Creed and to the Nicene Creed, and there is little doubt that these fundamental creeds operated effectively in that capacity.[34] However, even here the distinction must be drawn between the Truth itself and the church's formulations of it, so that in any proper appeal to a rule of faith in the credal sense, appeal must still be made to the Truth itself in its own substance and authority, the *Autoalētheia,* as the Greek fathers spoke of it. This is the theme to which we must now turn.

4.
Truth and Justification
in Doctrinal Formulation

Biblical interpretation and theological understanding clearly go hand in hand together. The Old Testament Scriptures arose out of the active self-revelation of God to mankind in the covenanted reciprocity which he established with the people of Israel for this very purpose, and the New Testament Scriptures grew out of the fulfillment of that divine revelation to mankind when in the fullness of time God incarnated his eternal Word in Jesus Christ in the midst of Israel. It is still through these Holy Scriptures that we are given knowledge of God, for we may not know him except in accordance with the steps he has taken to make himself known or through the means he has provided for his continuing self-revelation. On the other hand, since these Holy Scriptures are correlated to God's self-revelation in this unique way, they themselves may not be interpreted aright except in the light of the knowledge of God which he continues to mediate to us in and through them. But what happens when people disagree in their interpretation of the Bible or in their theological understanding of it? How are interpretations and theological ideas to be put to the test? Let it be granted that interpretation and theological understanding must keep within the semantic scope of the Scriptures and therefore with the general scope of faith to which they give rise in the church, but the question is still to the point, especially in view of disagreements that are not overcome merely by appeal to the Holy Scriptures.

That was the important issue raised by John Calvin in his preface to the *Institute* of 1536, which he addressed as an open letter to Francis I of France. He defended the doctrine set forth in it from the accusations of novelty and error and claimed that the exposition kept within the bounds prescribed by the Word of God and within the limits laid down by the ancient fathers of the church, who had based their doctrine upon that of the apostles. However, in view of the charge that appeal to the Word of God was no more than a pretext to put forward erroneous ideas, Calvin insisted that appeal must be made beyond all ecclesiastical authority or biblical citation to *the Truth of God,* for that is the supreme Authority to which all must submit and on which everyone must rely. Ultimately it is by reference to that Truth directly that judgment must be passed upon the truth or error of theological interpretation and statement.[1]

The principle that Calvin brought into play here was "accord with the analogy of faith" *(ad fidei analogiam)* or "accord with this rule of faith" *(ad hanc fidei regulam).* This is a critical movement of thought in which we test the fidelity of interpretation or doctrinal formulation by tracing our thought back to its source and ground in the reality known, that is, one in which we refer everything to God in accordance with his absolute priority and nothing to ourselves. To commit ourselves to God in faith in this way means that we let ourselves be called so radically in question that we are stripped of all our presuppositions and prejudgments. We let the Truth of God retain its own majesty *(suam dignitatem Dei veritas retineat)* in all our biblical interpretations and doctrinal formulations, for it constitutes a realm over which we can never exercise any rule or control. Ours is to listen to it and give heed to it. It is in this ultimate Truth of God, then, that authority resides, and not in those who seek to interpret it, or in a set of doctrines that might substitute for it—i.e., in a *regula fidei* in the other sense—for it is the Truth itself and not any formulation of the church's understanding of it that is the canon or criterion of true knowledge. The Truth of God may be known only in accordance with what it is independently in itself and as we on our part submit our understanding to its judgment.[2]

It must be noted that what Calvin has to say here is entirely consistent with the doctrine of justification by Grace, which means that in all our relations with God as moral or religious beings, we can never claim to have right or truth in ourselves, but may find our right and truth only in Christ. Applied to the task of theology, justification by Grace alone means that we may never claim the truth for our own statements, but must rather think of our statements as pointing away to Christ, who alone is the Truth. Theological statements do not carry their truth in themselves, but are true only insofar as they direct us away from themselves to the one Truth in God. Justification by the Grace of Christ alone, therefore, means that we may not boast of our orthodoxy or be dogmatic about our interpretations and formulations, for all we do is questionable and fallible. Understood in this epistemological way, justification by Grace, or verification through the Truth that Christ himself is, provides theology with the most powerful principle of objectivity, for it cuts away the ground from all our subjective claims and assertions.

This conception of truth is not peculiar to Calvin or to the Reformation, as he readily admitted, for he took it over from the theological tradition of the church as it developed from the Holy Scriptures. It is a conception which he shared particularly with Athanasius, Gregory of Nazianzus, and Cyril of Alexandria in the East, and with Hilary, Augustine, and Anselm of Canterbury in the West. In it, with the help of Greek thought, Old and New Testament strands were woven together. In the Old Testament, God is regarded as the Source and Standard of all truth, for he is himself the Truth, who keeps truth forever. The stress is upon the fact that God's Truth is his steadfastness and consistency, his reliability in being and action, but it is Truth that claims our acknowledgment and calls upon us responsibly to keep faith and truth with God and with one another. In the New Testament this tradition of thought is continued, but with the incarnation the stress is on the Truth in the form of personal Being revealed to us in Jesus Christ, for in him God is known to be in himself what he is in his unveiling toward us, while the Spirit of Truth is understood as the presence of God to us in his own Being, who enlightens us and leads us into all truth. Through this relation to God in Jesus Christ his incarnate Word, the ontological and intellectual aspects of truth, the truth of being and the truth of understanding, are held indivisibly together.

Now if we think of Jesus Christ in this way as the Truth in his own Person, our statements about him, biblical and theological statements, cannot be true in the same sense as Jesus Christ is true, for they do not have their truth in themselves but in their reference to him away from themselves, and they are true insofar as that reference is truthful and appropriate. By referring to him away from themselves, they both subordinate themselves to him and discriminate themselves from him. A semantic relation of this kind holds good, as we have seen, in any realist relation between statements and realities to which they refer. But if Jesus Christ is the ultimate Truth of God, as we believe him to be, then our statements about him, insofar as they are true, must refer to him accordingly, subjecting themselves to him and discriminating themselves from him in their utter difference from him as creaturely and contingent. But if it is asked how contingent statements can refer to what is utterly different from them, we must point back to the incarnation of the eternal Word and Truth of God in Jesus Christ, for in him the Word and Truth of God meet us within our creaturely and contingent world, where they are accessible to us and amenable to our statements.[3] The incarnation involves a hypostatic union not only between the Word of God and the word of man, the Rationality of God and the rationality of man, but between the uncreated Truth of God and the created truth of this world which God has made and to which we belong. Hence in Jesus Christ we have to reckon with one who is God's ultimate Truth and our contingent truth in the indivisible oneness of his personal Being, and therefore with one in whom God's ultimate Truth has become humanly articulate and communicable in words and truths within the reciprocities and intelligibilities of our contingent existence in space and time. Thus when our contingent statements refer away from themselves to the Truth of God as it is in Jesus Christ, they do not have to bridge the infinite difference between the creature and the Creator in order to terminate upon that Truth, for they may refer to it in its incarnate Reality, and insofar as they are true they may actually terminate upon that incarnate Reality and thus upon the Truth of God Almighty himself.

Since Jesus Christ in his own personal Being incarnates the Word and Truth of God, he concentrates in and through himself the self-revelation and self-communication of God to mankind. In Jesus Christ we come up against God's own personal Being, in which he bears directly upon us with the creative presence and power of ultimate Truth, authenticating and interpreting himself to us. Jesus Christ is that Truth truthfully communicating himself, and enabling us truthfully to receive him. He is the Truth communicating himself in and through truths, who does not communicate himself apart from truths, and who does not communicate truths apart from himself. It is in this utterly unique way that Jesus

Christ constitutes in himself the controlling and justifying Center of reference for all our statements about God, and as such he is the ultimate Judge of their truth or falsity. If we are adequately to appreciate what this implies for doctrinal formulation, we must clarify our understanding of the uniqueness of the Truth as it is in Jesus Christ, that is, Truth as Word and Act and Being in the indivisible oneness of his divine-human Person—for appropriate interpretation and understanding on our part of the Truth as it is in Jesus Christ must surely be in accordance with his unique nature. It is in and through Jesus Christ alone, what he was and did and said as the incarnate Truth, that we are put in the right with the Truth of God. Hence all our statements about the Truth will have their validity or truthfulness only through their derivation from and congruence with him as their Source and Justification.

By way of opening up the field for a closer examination of what the identity of Jesus Christ with the Truth means for the enunciation and verification of theological statements, let us first turn our attention to the different levels on which we have to reckon with questions of truth, the truth of statements and the truth of created being, both of which are contingent, and the supreme self-sufficient Truth of God. It will be helpful to take our cue from the elegant discussion of these distinctions offered by Anselm, especially in the *De veritate,* [4] and to develop what is relevant in his presentation for our purpose here.

In line with the patristic tradition (which, as we have seen, also lay behind Calvin's thought), Anselm meant by *truth* the reality of things as they actually are and as they show themselves to be, and therefore as they ought to be known and expressed by us. Everything is, under God, what it actually is and not something else, and cannot be other than it is. Therefore everything must be discerned and apprehended in accordance with the necessity of its being what it is or the impossibility of its being otherwise. To the "solid truth" or necessity in the object of knowledge there corresponds a truth or necessity in knowledge, the impossibility of conceiving the object rightly as being other than it is. Hence all interpretation and understanding of conceptions and statements must be critically tested through a concurrent activity in which we listen in to the truth of things, yielding to their inherent necessity, for in that way we are enabled to straighten out conceptions and statements in accordance with the nature of things as they really are.

In the *De veritate* Anselm put forward a brief definition of truth as "rightness" *(rectitudo)*. He evidently had in mind the patristic custom (influenced by Plato's *Cratylus*) of thinking of concepts and terms as rightly *(orthōs, recte)* related to the realities they signify when they bear upon them not in a conventional but in a real or natural way. With the help of this definition he analyzed what is meant by truth, distinguishing between the truth of signification, the truth of things, and the supreme Truth of God, and showing that they build a semantic structure in which the truth of signification depends on the truth of things, and the truth of things depends on the Supreme Truth, which depends on nothing, for it is completely self-subsistent. Thus all truths point back to the one Supreme Truth, and it is ultimately only in the light of that Truth that one can speak of the truth of signification or the truth of being.

1. *The Truth of signification* is that which must be signified of a thing in accordance with its nature. Since a thing is what it is and not another thing, we signify it rightly when we signify it in accordance with what it is. We owe it to the nature of the thing to do that. We signify it truly when we fulfill an obligation *(debitum)* toward the reality signified. This is what we have in mind when we say that a statement is true, when it signifies as it ought by stating what is the case. The truth of a statement, then, is not lodged in the

statement itself, but is its rightness in a relation to the thing signified. By this Anselm means an objective rightness, one that remains when the signification itself perishes, for it derives from the rightness of the reality to which it refers, and shows through when it is signified rightly, although it is not affected by the signification itself.

Anselm draws a distinction, however, between two "truths" of statement, since there are two respects in which a statement can be said to do what it ought, and thus a statement can have two rightnesses. A statement has a truth or rightness when it fulfills a syntactic function as a consistent and coherent set of words, irrespective of whether what it says is true or false. (Anselm admits that we do not usually speak of a statement as "true" in this way.) And a statement has a truth or rightness when it fulfills a semantic function in referring to a state of affairs beyond itself. Unless a statement has a truth in the first respect, i.e., makes verbal sense, it cannot be employed meaningfully to refer to a state of affairs. If it has truth in the second respect, however, its truth or rightness will depend on the truth or rightness of that which it undertakes to signify. Properly speaking, then, a statement is true when it is true in both respects, that is, when a statement that makes verbal sense is employed in such a way that it refers rightly to a state of affairs beyond itself. This is what Anselm called the truth of signification, in which both poles of signification have their place, with a rightness in the signifying statement and a rightness in its relation to the thing signified. However, since this rightness depends on the nature of the thing signified, the truth of signification cannot stand by itself but follows as effect from a rightness in the thing signified.

2. *The truth of things* is their being what they are and ought to be according to their natures. When they are what they ought to be, they are rightly, and that rightness of their being remains whether we know it or not. It is independent

and immutable, unaffected by the truth of signification. Anselm therefore defines the truth of a thing in terms of its essence, its being what it is, and its necessity, its inability to be other than it is. However, this truth or rightness of being in created things is not immanent or self-subsistent in them as such, but is in them only so far as they are truly or rightly related to their source in the supreme Being, who only is self-subsistent. That is to say, in virtue of its contingent nature the truth of created being points beyond itself to the eternal Truth of God, which is its Ground and Cause. Thus, just as the truth of signification fulfills a *debitum* exacted from it by a rightness in the thing signified and can be spoken of as its effect, so the truth or rightness of being in the thing signified arises out of the fact that it is what it ought to be in relation to the supreme Truth and is thus to be regarded as the effect caused by the supreme Truth in the nature or essence of created things. It is in this rightness of created or contingent being that Anselm finds the objective truth of signification, and by the same token he finds an objective signification in created or contingent things themselves, since by being what they are they signify that they are grounded beyond themselves in the eternal Truth of God. It is their obligatory relation to the Truth of God that gives them their objectivity and in fact deepens that objectivity indefinitely.

3. *The supreme Truth of God* is the ultimate or transcendent Rightness of God's own self-subsistent and self-sufficient Being. There is a fundamental difference between divine Truth or Rightness and all other truth or rightness, for while the rightness of signification and the rightness of being are what they are obliged to be, the supreme Truth is not Rightness because it has any obligation. Everything else is under obligation to it, but the supreme Truth is under obligation to nothing, nor is it what it is for any other reason than that it is. Thus the Truth of God is the Source and Ground of

all other truths and is itself caused by nothing outside of himself. Under the supreme Truth, then, the Truth of all truth, some truths are only effects, while others are causes as well as effects. Thus the truth that is in the existence of contingent beings is both the effect of the supreme Truth and the cause of the truths of thought and statement, but the truths of thought and statement are in no sense causes of other truths. All truths point back to the supreme Truth, and it is ultimately only in the light of that Truth that one can speak of the truth of signification or the truth of being. Hence the transcendent reference of our conceptions and statements to and beyond the truth of being belongs to the full scope of the truth of signification.

This analysis of the relation of dependence between the truth of signification and the truth of being, and between the truth of being and the supreme Truth, is very important. It shows the impropriety of reducing the truth of statement simply to its truth-function in discourse and discloses the objective depth that a true statement must have beyond itself. In other words, it calls in question the fallacious tendency to pass from the truth of being to the truth of signification and then to the truth of composition, which has the effect of substituting syntactic validity for semantic truth. Anselm sought to assert with the greatest force the ontological priority and objectivity of truth. He insisted that the truth of signification is not only the conformity of statement to the reality stated, but an obligatory conformity, for the statement is enunciated under the claim or demand that comes from the side of what is stated, and it is made in acknowledgment of that claim and in accordance with the nature of the reality that stands behind it. This means that there is an irreversible relation between the sign and the thing signified, the statement and the reality stated, for the truth of human statements is the consequence of the existence of things. But the objectivity is even deeper, for the truth of the existence of things follows similarly from the Truth of God himself, since those things not only are what they actually are, but are what they are under the compulsion that derives from God himself.

Practically speaking, this means that interpretation and understanding operate with a twofold truth, the truth of signification and the truth of being. Statements are rightly interpreted when they are understood in their compulsory reference to the things signified, and when those things signified are understood for what they are and for what in accordance with their natures they must be. But when we see that the rightness of being points beyond, to a source of being in the supreme Being, then we see that the truer statements are, the more they are open toward the ultimate Truth. By their very nature, then, true statements have an indefinite quality about them which they acquire through pointing to the infinite and eternal Truth of God. This applies above all to theological statements, for they are statements about God, than whom none greater can be conceived, the God who infinitely transcends our thoughts and statements about him. Therefore statements about him are rightly made and are rightly interpreted when we respect "the rationality of the Truth that is so wide and so profound that it cannot possibly be exhausted by mortals," as Anselm says.[5]

Now in order to get the full benefit of Anselm's analysis for the interpretation, understanding, and formulation of theological truth, we must take into account the fact, on which Anselm enlarges in various works, that fundamental forms of speech *(locutio)* and of thought or rationality *(ratio)* belong to the truth on all three levels. We must bear in mind here that in his realist view of language, Anselm held that we operate with a basic form of word or speech which is objectively determined by the reality denoted. This is the "natural" word (the *verbum rei,* as he regularly called it), which does not vary but is the primary and proper word that underlies all variations in different languages. It is in and through this basic form of word that speech really does its work in ostensive acts that lead to the recognition of the objects concerned. It is so related to the reality denoted that in and through it the reality itself comes to view.[6] In line with this, Anselm held that corresponding to the truth of signification and the truth of things there is a basic form of speech about things *(locutio rerum)* at work in signification which depends on and is governed by an objective form of speech in things *(intima locutio rerum)*. But that in its turn points back to an ultimate form of speech in God himself *(locutio intima apud summam substantiam)*, an active speech *(locutio rerum)* which is both the means through which things were created and the means, once they were created, through which they may be known. Behind this, of course, lies the biblical teaching that all things that are made are created through the Word of God, and they remain in existence in that they consist in and continue to be upheld by the Word of the Creator. That is to say, the language of creation—the object-language found in all contingent realities—goes back to the creative speaking of God himself, and it is only as we give ear to that creative speaking in God that we may understand the rational order which he has conferred on the universe and all its immanent processes and connections.

The realism with which Anselm understands this creative speech in God, to which all the basic forms of speech embedded in created realities go back, has the effect of reinforcing his stress upon the ontological priority and objectivity of truth in all genuine knowledge. Since things are known truly through an inner speech that derives from and is backed up by a speech in God himself, we may make statements about them that are genuinely objective. But we may make statements like that only when we penetrate into the inner speech of created things and let it govern our speech about them. That is to say, the form that these realities take in our knowledge of them is not one that we invent and impose upon them, but one which we discern in them and seek to express in corresponding statements about them. But when we ask how we are to think of this objective speech as embedded in created beings, and therefore in what sense they may be said to speak to us and reveal their natures, Anselm points to the fact that cognate to their inner speech created realities also have a basic form of rationality which they derive likewise from the uncreated Rationality of the supreme Truth. Parallel, then, to the three levels of truth and of basic forms of speech we must take into account three levels of rationality, for there is a basic form of rationality which in different ways manifests itself in the truth of signification, the truth of being, and in the Supreme Truth. Here we have to envisage the same hierarchic structure in which the rationality of the lower level depends on and is controlled by the rationality of the higher level, while the internal rationality of the whole structure points to and requires the ultimate transcendent Rationality of God as its creative ground and sufficient reason.

Hence, in answer to the question of how we are to think of the inner speech of created realities as speaking to us and revealing their natures, Anselm points out that we must penetrate into their inner rationality, and allow our understanding to be informed and guided by it, and seek to articulate that in an orderly and rational manner. We allow the truth of reality to force itself upon us in its own inherent rationality, and we establish our knowledge through the development of necessary reasons derived from the reality being investigated. But what else is this but to give ear to the inner speech in the creaturely reality, and to translate it into an appropriate language of our own? It is through laying bare the ontological reasons in things that we allow them to speak to us and disclose themselves to us as they are and as they should be, i.e., in their truth. But in so doing we know them not just as they are in themselves but as they ought to be in the supreme Truth, that is, in a dimension of rationality and objectivity that reaches out far beyond them into God and is backed up by his creative Word.

Now if human statements about created realities are true insofar as they derive from and bear upon an objective speech embedded in them that goes back to the creative Word of God, how much more must that be the case with true human statements about God! They derive their rational content and their truth through a speech which God has provided for us in the Holy Scriptures, but a speech that goes back to the eternal Word of God consubstantial with himself. True human statements about God are made, therefore, in obedient response to speech directed to man by God, so that the rational articulation that these statements involve takes place on the basis of a speech of God that has been heard, believed, and understood by man. However, just as the truth of signification derives from the truth in the essential natures of created things (although that in turn is the effect of the supreme Truth), and just as the inner rationality of our knowledge derives from an objective rationality in the nature of created realities (although that also is one conferred upon them with their creation and points back to its source in the uncreated Rationality of God), so the inner speech of theological statements derives from and depends on the words and acts of God in his self-revelation, yet they are created forms or representations of the Word of God addressed to us. It is because the inner speech of theological statements goes back through the inner speech of biblical statements, which is their mediate source, to an eternal speech in God himself that those statements, when true, enshrine a conceptuality or rationality that is objectively rooted and grounded in God's own self-revelation, and is not just constructed out of man's own independent interpretation and understanding. They are objectively determined expressions or formulations, compellingly related to the Word or inner speech of God mediated to man through the Holy Scriptures through which God continues to address us.

Let us return to the point that the different levels of truth, speech, and rationality are hierarchically ordered in a semantic focus that points to and is overarched by the transcendent Truth, Speech, and Rationality of God in his self-evidencing reality and creative power. This means that in seeking to interpret biblical statements and formulate doctrinal statements of our own on that basis, we must penetrate through the created truth, speech, and rationality of biblical statements to the solid ground of the Truth, Speech, and Rationality of God upon which they rest, in order that everything may be understood and expounded directly in the light of the Truth that God himself is, under his constant guidance, and in conformity to the structures of rationality or conceptuality which we are given when we listen to that Truth and submit our minds to its compelling claims. This is not to resist or impugn the authority of the Holy Scriptures, but on the contrary to let them serve the ultimate Authority of God himself, to which they direct us. Faith and certainty do not rest on biblical authority as such, far less on ecclesiastical authority, but on the solid truth that underlies all the teaching of the Holy Scriptures. Christian theology arises properly out of a compulsive thinking and speaking face to face with the God revealed to us through the Holy Scriptures, for its real content is not the signifying truths of the Scriptures but the Truth of God revealed in and through them. What must guide theological statements is certainly the truth content of the Scriptures, but what must determine theological formulation is the objective truth forced upon the interpreter of the Scriptures by God himself. Hence, far from leaving the realm of the Holy Scriptures, where knowledge of God is actually mediated to us, we remain within it so that we may bring our minds directly under the compulsion of the Truth of God and the impress of his Rationality. We are thereby enabled both to do greater justice to the Holy Scriptures and to formulate our own theological statements with greater depth and sharper precision.

Our discussion of Anselm's clarifying analysis of truth and its contribution to the task of Christian theology may have given the impression that it is all a severely intellectualist enterprise, but that is far from being the case, and it would certainly not do justice to Anselm. The very fact so relentlessly emphasized by Anselm, that both in interpretation and theological formulation we are brought face to face with God in his own ultimate Truth and Reality, means that we cannot undertake these tasks without a living, personal experience of that Truth, and without constant prayer that we may be given illumination to understand and ability to speak of the Truth which by its ultimate nature is utterly beyond us.[7] Since theological activity is concerned with knowledge of God in this way, it can take place only within a reciprocal relation or communion in which God himself is not only the object of knowledge but in a profound sense he who condescends to be one with us in our creaturely condition in order to sustain our knowing of him from below and match it to himself. This is precisely what we are now to consider: the fact that the Ultimate Truth of God has become incarnate in our world of contingent being and encounters us there in such a way that he shares and gathers up into himself, in his relation as Man on earth to God the Father in heaven, the whole structure of truth, from the truth of signification through the truth of being to the supreme Truth of God, and thus constitutes for us at every level of truth both the controlling and integrating center of reference and the reality of its anchorage in God.

The comprehensive significance of this incarnation of God's Truth in our contingent existence is made very clear in the words of Jesus as they are reported to us by The Gospel According to John: "I am the Way, the Truth, and the Life: no one comes to the Father, but by me" (John 14:6). Here we have the majestic *I am* of the self-subsistent Truth of God meeting us face to face on our side of the creature/Creator relationship and addressing us in a human statement which signifies the Truth that Jesus Christ himself is in our created being, and which at the same time refers us back in and through himself to God the Father. Thus in him the truth of signification, the truth of created being, and the ultimate Truth of God, without being confused, are indivisibly united in the oneness of his divine-human Person, and it is as such that he is the self-revelation and self-communication of God to us in space and time. In this statement Jesus Christ is communicating truth about himself and God the Father, but it is not just truth that he is communicating in these words but himself in and through that truth. He is not just someone speaking about the Truth, but the very Truth of God uttering himself in a human statement, and yet in such a way as Man on earth before God that he constitutes in himself the perfect response of man to the self-communication of the Truth of God. He is at one and the same time Truth from God to man and truth from man to God, and as such he is the standard and norm for the formulation of all truth about God and his interaction with man.

In claiming to be the *Way*, Jesus Christ pointed to himself in his own personal reality and historical particularity as providing mankind with definitive access to God the Father. He is not simply a Teacher who has come from God to tell us about the way, for he is in his own personal Being the Way to which he refers. As the one Mediator between God and man, the Man Christ Jesus both concentrates the self-revelation of God and concentrates our response to that revelation in himself. This has the effect of determining the bounds of theological inquiry by binding it to the actual ground of God's self-communication in the incarnation, thereby prohibiting it from straying into timeless and spaceless generalities or abstract possibilities; but it also has the effect of correlating theological concepts to the personal Being of Jesus Christ himself, thereby precluding theological inquiry from sliding into a formalistic manipulation of truths uncontrolled by the substance of God's self-signification and self-interpretation in Jesus. In claiming to be the *Truth,* Jesus Christ pointed to himself as the self-authenticating Truth of God who communicates himself in and through truths, who does not communicate himself apart from truths, but who does not communicate truths apart from himself. As the decisive embodiment of God's Truth he is also the authoritative Judge of all that claims to be truth. All divine judgment has been committed by the Father to him, so that all men are judged in their reaction to Jesus Christ as the Truth. This has the effect of giving theological activity a critical edge, for face to face with Jesus Christ the ultimate Truth of God incarnate, it cannot take refuge in neutrality but must submit all its doctrinal formulations to him as the Judge of their truth or falsity. In claiming to be the *Life,* Jesus Christ pointed to himself as the actualization among men of the creative Life of God and therefore as the sole Source of life and salvation for mankind. As the incarnate presence of the living God in space and time, he presents himself to our faith as its living dynamic Object. This has the effect of calling for a living theology, a way of thinking which is at the same time a way of living, that cannot be abstracted from the life-giving acts of Christ in the depths of human being and must therefore affect man radically in his daily life and activity. It is a responsible way of thinking in which we are ontologically and personally committed to God and for which we have to give an account to God in our life within the church and its mission in the world. Since Jesus Christ, then, is the one Way which God himself has taken in his self-revelation and self-communication to mankind, he constitutes in himself as the Way, the Truth, and the Life the one exclusive approach to God the Father whereby we may have real access to him.

At the very heart of this self-presentation of Jesus Christ as the Truth—"I am the Truth"—there is something which we must now consider in greater depth, for it has very far-reaching implications for Christian theology, the identity of the Truth with the personal Being of Christ. That is to say, we have to reckon with the intense personalization of the Truth. This does not mean that the Truth of God which he eternally is was not personal before he became incarnate, for in God himself there is an inexhaustible fullness of Personal Being, with which we are concerned in the doctrine of the Holy Trinity and which lies behind all that we have to think and say here. We cannot enter into that now, but the point that demands our attention is that, with the incarnation of the Truth in Jesus Christ within the structure of our interpersonal human relations where we are persons through onto-relations with one another, an intense personalization of God's self-manifestation toward us has taken place which calls for a correspondingly intense personalization of our relations with God. It is not only that the Truth meets us in the form of personal Being but that he meets us in the form of personal Being who is personal in his own right. Strictly speaking, as Karl Barth has pointed out, God alone is Person in the full and proper sense, for he is the one self-subsistent Person from whom all that is personal derives.[8] We are persons only through derivation from him and in dependence on him, persons in a very real if secondary sense, but God himself is person-constituting

Person. That is the way in which the Truth meets us in Jesus Christ, as personalizing Person. In him the Truth communicates himself to us, not without truths to be sure, but in and through all truths, as Truth in the form of personalizing Being.

Let us note right way that this entails a radical inverting of the knowing relationship, which is unlike anything that we experience elsewhere. In all normal epistemic acts we the knowing subjects are in control of our knowing operations when the object of our knowledge is epistemically on a lower level, although personally it may be on the same level as ourselves. Here, however, we do not know the Truth by occupying a level above it or by relation to it on the same level as ourselves, and certainly not by looking down on it, for this is the ultimate person-constituting Truth of the Lord God to whom we may only look up in reverent obedience and worship and thanksgiving.[9] We may know him only as we are known by him and are turned inside out in such a way that the controlling center of ourselves is transferred from ourselves to Christ—that is, only as we yield ourselves to the creative impact of his self-communication and as the subjective pole of our knowing relation is radically transformed and informed by the objective personalizing pole of the Truth of God himself.[10] To know the Truth of God as he encounters us in Jesus Christ in the form of personalizing Being entails a profound conversion or restructuring of our own personal being in mind and will and life, which cannot but affect the basic position that we adopt in all theological interpretation and formulation.

While we cannot offer here a full account of what this understanding of Truth implies for theological activity, it may be sufficient to consider several respects in which it bears directly upon our present purpose.

1. *The Truth of God retains his own essential mystery even in the midst of his self-revelation.* While God reveals and com-

municates himself to us in the historical reality and particularity of Jesus Christ, the Truth that he is in Jesus Christ his incarnate Son, and eternally in himself the Father, remains infinitely transcendent. It is the revelation of Truth so unlimited and inexhaustible that the more we know of him the more we realize the ineffable and infinite fullness of his Reality which defies complete disclosure within the limits of our contingent being and experience. On the other hand, this is not unintelligible Mystery, for while it reaches out indefinitely beyond our apprehension it increasingly throws light upon ever-wider areas of knowledge and experience. God's Mystery expresses the objective depth of his Intelligibility, the infinite excess of his uncreated Rationality over our created rationality. Thus from the point of view of our experience of the Truth, mystery means that our knowledge is of far more than we can ever specify or reduce to clear-cut —that is, delimited—conceptions or propositions, and is concerned with a fullness of meaning which by its very nature resists and eludes all attempts to reduce it without remainder, as it were, to what we can formulate or systematize. Or, to put it otherwise, mystery means that behind the objectivities and intelligibilities of this spatiotemporal universe in which the Truth of God discloses himself to us, there is an infinite depth of Reality calling for recognition and reverence, openness of mind and wonder toward it. There is an ultimate Objectivity which cannot be disclosed within the creaturely objectivities through which we encounter him, but the creaturely objectivities have their meaning through this relation in referential depth to that Objectivity which infinitely transcends them.

That precisely is the objective Truth of God whom we meet in Jesus Christ, for what God is antecedently and eternally in himself he really is toward us in the concrete embodiment of his Truth in Jesus Christ the Word made flesh. As we have seen, in Jesus Christ God has so communicated himself to us in our humanity that human words are taken to speak for God, and therefore it is in and through Jesus Christ that our human words may rightly and properly speak of God—insofar, that is, as they are rooted in the Mystery of Christ the incarnate Truth. Thus theological statements must derive from and be grounded in the articulate intelligibility of Jesus Christ the eternal Word made flesh, and they must refer to the Truth embodied in his divine-human personal Being as the controlling center of their reference to God and the objective basis on which they rely for their own truth as statements about God. In order to do this, however, theological statements must refer away from themselves as signifying operations to the Truth of Being in Jesus Christ and be made in and through him to terminate upon the ultimate Truth of God the Father. It is of the utmost importance for us both in biblical interpretation and in doctrinal formulation to recognize that the Word or Truth of God incarnate in the personal Being of Jesus Christ is far more than can be made articulate in verbal or conceptual form. The very fact that God has incarnated his Word or Truth in Jesus Christ in this way means that Jesus Christ is God's self-articulation, and that merely verbal or conceptual expressions are inadequate in themselves but adequately fulfill their given function when they direct us away from themselves to the objective self-signification of God's Truth in Jesus Christ. If even Jesus Christ the Son of God become man points us from himself to God the Father, how much more do the biblical witnesses and testimonies point us away from themselves to Christ and in and through him to God? *A fortiori* we must take with utter seriousness the fact that theological statements and formulations, far from containing their truth in themselves, point away from themselves to God in Jesus Christ as their sole truth and justification.

This transcendence of the Word or Truth of God in Jesus

Christ over all verbal or conceptual expression of him should become indubitably clear to us through a consideration of the utterly unique fact that the Truth, Word, and Act of God coinhere inseparably in one another in the personal Being of Jesus Christ. As for us, our words and acts are in addition to what we are and they pass away even when we remain. In Jesus Christ this is not the case. His Word is his Person in communication, for in speaking his Word he himself is personally present in the Word communicating himself. He is no less personal because he is in Person identical with his Word, and his Word is not less Word because he is in his Word identical with his Person. On the contrary, his Word is truly and properly Word and his Person is truly and properly Person in this identification. He is Person, but not in the derived sense in which we are persons, as we have seen, for he is person-constituting or personalizing Person. That is to say, in what he is and what he says he is creative Act of God, so that we have to think of him as Person and as Word only in an active sense, for his Word does not fall short of what he is or does, and his Person does not remain uncommitted in his Act any more than he is uncommitted in his Word. But we must also bring the Truth of God into this coinherence in Christ, for it belongs to the very nature of God's Truth that he is at once Person, and Word, and Act. He is personal Being and yet communicable Truth, but communicable Truth that belongs to the identity of his Word and Act, and thus he is self-authenticating, self-fulfilling, and self-actualizing Truth, the creative Truth of God.

The very fact that God communicates to us not just truths about himself but his very Self in this way, in the personal and personalizing Being of Jesus Christ, makes it clear that the Word or Truth of God transcends all conceptual or verbal articulation of truth about him. Insofar as these articulations are true they indicate far more than they can express. Human statements, even biblical statements, signifying the Truth of God as it is in Jesus Christ are themselves contingent and perishable, but their objective signification in the Word or Truth of God remains, for he is what he is independent of them. Epistemologically this is quite consistent with what we have found to be the proper, realist functioning of words and statements. Of course the objective signification in created being to which true statements refer is perishable likewise, but that signification, like all the language conferred on the creation by the Creator, points beyond itself to the creative signification in the ultimate Truth of God which is its eternal and unchanging Ground, so that it is within the semantic scope constituted by that ultimate reference that all signification on the lower levels of reality has its justification.

Since biblical statements indicate more than they can signify at any time, and more than we can express in our interpretation of them, they manifest a predictive quality, for they point above and beyond themselves to the inexhaustible Truth of God. A faithful interpretation of biblical statements, therefore, will not cut short their transcendent reference but will seek to allow their implications to disclose themselves in the light of that reference. However, there is no formal or hermeneutical way of anticipating such a disclosure in the future on the ground of what has already been disclosed, for precisely the same reason, namely, that biblical statements indicate far more than they can express. The ultimate Truth of God to which they point beyond themselves is so unlimited in his intelligibility and freedom that he breaks through the calculus of our predictions and keeps on disclosing himself in quite unexpected ways. There is, therefore, a continuously surprising, unpredictable element in biblical statements which they have through their correlation with the ultimate Truth of God which will always exceed what can be thought or said of him. It is precisely because biblical statements signify an objective truth independent of them which will not behave according to prediction that we may rest assured that they are in genuine contact with the transcendent Truth and Reality of God. Insofar as theological statements and formulations are grounded in God's self-revelation through the Holy Scriptures, they will manifest qualities corresponding to those of biblical statements, in indicating far more than they can articulate. They will manifest a persistent fertility in serving a deeper and richer apprehension of the truth than they did when they were first formulated, but they will maintain an essentially open structure correlated to the transcendent power of the Truth embodied in Jesus Christ to disclose himself in quite surprising and unsuspected ways in the future. Hence we must take it to be the mark of true theological statements that they are harnessed to an objective signification of the Truth of God in Jesus Christ which far outstrips all our conceptions and formulations while nevertheless providing them with the force of their truth.

2. *The truth of theological statements is to be found not in themselves but in the truthfulness of their relation to the realities they signify.* A distinction must be drawn, therefore, between truth and truthfulness, between what is true in itself in its own independent right and what is true in virtue of a relation to truth beyond itself. We recall again at this point Anselm's clarifying account of several levels of truth, the truth of signifying statement, the truth of created being, and the supreme Truth, and the fact that the two lower levels of truth are open upward to the supreme Truth of God, who in his own self-subsistent, immutable Reality provides them with their ultimate ground of justification and their objective force. The truth is such that whether we find it in created being or divine Being, it lays us under a debt: we owe it to the truth to be truly related to it. While truthfulness involves an obligatory reference back to the truth of

being, the truth of being retains its ontological priority, for it is what it is in its own reality before it is acknowledged by us, and what it is in itself is the compulsive ground of our recognition of it and the source of our conceiving of it and the controlling center of our statements about it. In theological thought and statement, the obligatory relation between the lower levels and the higher is immensely reinforced through the incarnate presence of the supreme Truth in Jesus Christ, in whom the truths of signification and created being are taken up and intimately coordinated to God's Truth through an intensely personalizing structure of reference and participation.

It is clearly essential to the truthfulness of theological concepts and statements that they distinguish themselves from the Truth of God, who has laid them under obligation to him, and that they direct us away from themselves to him as their Source and Ground. In discriminating themselves from the Truth in this way, theological concepts and statements also testify to their own inadequacy or defectiveness, or, as Calvin used to say, they disclose a measure of "impropriety" in themselves.[11] They intend a Reality beyond their creaturely content by which their creaturely content is shown to be inadequate. They would not be truthful if they failed to do that, for then they would put themselves on the same level as the Truth they signify and confound the truth of signification with the truth of being. However, we must not be alarmed at the measure of disparity or impropriety between theological concepts or statements and the Truth they are employed to signify, for they are not for that reason necessarily false. Since their function is primarily denotative in pointing to the Truth away from themselves, it is precisely that disparity or impropriety which helps us not to confound them with the realities they intimate and thus serves their denotative purpose. Since concepts and statements function in this way, we use them rightly and truly when we do not let our understanding stop short at the concepts or statements themselves, but pass through them to think and speak of the realities to which they direct our understanding. We may use them rightly or truly in this way insofar as we allow them to serve the self-revelation of God and to receive the imprint of his creative Word. Granted, then, that the forms of thought and speech of our doctrinal formulations fall far short of what they intend, and therein reveal the considerable measure of their inadequacy, nevertheless under the creative impact of the Word upon them they are enabled beyond their natural capacity to focus our minds upon God's own Truth so that we may think and speak of him on the free ground of his own self-evidencing Being and Reality.

Now it is worth noting that we can be truthful toward what is false as well as what is true, for we "do justice" to falsehood when we think and speak of it as false and not otherwise. In this case, however, in a so-called "honest to God" relation, truthfulness is subjectively and not objectively controlled, but when we are truthful toward what is independently true, truthfulness is objectively controlled. In this case, truthfulness is a genuine form of truth grounded in a true state of affairs beyond itself. To be true, therefore, theological statements must both be truthful and be rooted in the truth itself, the truth of created being or the ultimate Truth of God. That is to say, both poles of the referring relation have their place, with a rightness in the referring statement and a rightness in the reality to which reference is made, but since the latter rightness depends on the nature of the reality referred to, its rightness or truth follows—in Anselm's way of speaking—as the "effect" of the reality referred to. The truthfulness of theological statements, therefore, depends not on the truthfulness of their intention but on a participation in the Truth which God alone can give.

In other words, theological concepts and statements have their justification through the Grace of God alone. They have their proper right and their proper truth, not through some process of verification which we put into effect by linking them to a ground in our prior knowledge, far less to some vaunted "self-understanding" on our part, as though we could compel God to be the truth of what we think and say of him, but solely through the self-giving of God in Jesus Christ, the Way and the Truth and the Life. Justification by the Grace of God in Jesus Christ has an epistemological as well as an ethical application. Just as the gracious self-giving of God calls in question all forms of moral self-justification on our part, so it calls in question all forms of epistemic self-verification on our part. By the very act of putting us freely in the Right and Truth of God, justification tells us that we are in untruth. To seek verification on any other ground than that which God has freely provided for us is to falsify the gospel at its very basis, no less than to seek moral justification on any other ground than that which he has freely provided in the Righteousness of Christ. Hence justification or verification by the Grace of God's Truth alone brings us with all our preconceptions and prior knowledge radically into question. By being put in the truth with God we are told that Jesus Christ is our Truth, that we have to look away from ourselves, our concepts and formulations, to him alone, and that therefore we dare not boast of a truth of our own. This applies, however, not only to all prior knowledge, for at every point in our ongoing theological thinking and speaking we have to let our knowledge, our theology, our doctrinal formulations, be called into question by the very Christ toward whom they point, for he alone is their proper Truth.

Quite clearly, the doctrine of justification immensely reinforces the point that we have been considering, that theological concepts and statements are truthful when they do not claim to have truth in themselves but point away from themselves to Christ the one Truth of God. Therefore whenever we claim that our doctrinal formulations have their truth in themselves, we are turning back into the way of self-justification. Out of sheer respect for the Majesty of the Truth of God as he reveals himself to us in the Holy Scriptures, we must do our utmost to think and speak faithfully and correctly about him on the basis of his self-revelation—that is the meaning of orthodoxy and humility before God. But when we have done all that it is our duty to do in these ways, we have still to confess that we are unprofitable servants, and that all our own efforts to think and speak truly of God fall short of his Truth. Far from looking for justification on the ground of our "orthodoxy," we can only serve the Truth faithfully or truthfully if we point away from ourselves and our statements to Christ himself. He who boasts of his orthodoxy sins against justification by Christ alone, for he justifies himself by appeal to the truth of his own beliefs or formulations of belief and thereby sets himself in conflict with the Truth and Grace of Christ.

3. *Theological statements and formulations have their freedom in the service of truth over which they have no control.* We should rather say that it is in the service of the ultimate Truth of God that theologians have their proper freedom in theological inquiry and in the formulation of Christian doctrine. Traditionally freedom has been defined, at least in modern times, in relation to the will as free will. But when we come to think of it, especially in the context of the gospel, this is a strange sort of freedom in which we are quite unable through free will to escape from our self-will or from imprisonment in our own self-centeredness, which through original sin has become so obdurately and inveterately ingrained in us. Instead of a subjectively controlled freedom, therefore, we should have in view an objectively controlled freedom, freedom that arises in interaction with a controlling

center beyond ourselves, such as that in which we participate when we love others objectively for their sake and not
for our own sake. This is the kind of freedom that comes
from the service of the Truth, for it is the Truth, as Jesus
taught, that makes us free (John 8:32). It is in and through
obligation to transcendent Truth over which we have no
control that we are made open to the Truth and are liber-
ated from incarceration in ourselves, and are thereby also
made open to the world of things and other selves around
us, that is, free for them.

We are familiar with a relation of this kind between freedom and truth in scientific inquiry and in scientific institutions. It has become increasingly clear in the realist orientation of science, before which necessitarian and positivist
ways of thought have had to be set aside, that freedom of
thought and the authority of realities characterized by an
intelligibility independent of our knowledge of them, freedom in pursuit of research and submission to universal laws
grounded in the intrinsic order of the universe, are intimately connected together in our openness to the disclosure
of new truths. As Michael Polanyi, for example, has shown
us, it is in commitment to the transcendent reality of truth
over which we have no control, in acknowledgment of transcendent obligations, and in dedication to transcendent
ideals which we affirm with universal intent that we have
our freedom as rational beings.[12] Personal acts of will and
decision are of course involved, but in response to the demands of truth which we cannot in good conscience or
reason avoid or refuse. "The freedom of the subjective
person to do as he pleases is overruled by the freedom of
the responsible person to act as he must." That is to say,
the freedom with which we are concerned in science is not
the freedom we try to exercise in the assertion of our own
autonomy or self-legislative will, but the openness of being
and thought that comes with the acceptance of the authority

of objectively and independently grounded truth. Moreover, in surrendering to its claims upon us we are delivered from the arbitrary control of unwarranted presuppositions and hidden prejudices in ourselves and the social culture to which we belong. To know and love and serve the truth objectively for its own sake is to be genuinely free. It is with that kind of freedom interlocked with authority that the integrity of science is bound up.

Formally this relation between the freedom of thought and statement and the authority of truth is not different in theological science, but there are differences due to the divine and personal nature of the Truth. Here also personal acts of will in commitment and decision with an objectively —not a subjectively—induced and controlled openness or freedom are in place. However, since these acts arise within the intensely personal reciprocity established through God's utterly free communication of himself to mankind in Jesus Christ, their personal nature and their openness or freedom are very much richer, and since they are made in response to the compelling claims of the ultimate Truth of God incarnate in Jesus Christ, they are subject to and grounded in the supreme self-subsistent Authority or Freedom *(exousia, autoexousia)* of the Lord God. Since the freedom we are concerned with here in theological thought and statement is creaturely or contingent, it is limited; but it is not less freedom because it is limited, for that which limits it, the transcendent Freedom or Authority of God, is the Ground of its freedom as creaturely or contingent. The interconnection between freedom and authority is altogether deepened and intensified in Jesus Christ, for in him contingent freedom and divine Freedom, created truth and uncreated Truth, are profoundly interlocked, and it is as such that he is both the creative Ground and the controlling Center for all our thought and statements about God.

Now since God reveals himself to us in and through the

created order of the spatiotemporal world, our knowledge of him is inevitably coordinated to the contingent objectivities and intelligibilities of that world. The latter have a critical significance for our knowledge and speech about God, for they provide the consistent structure of order on which our human concepts and statements rely in significant and truthful communication with one another, and as such they constitute the given medium for the self-revelation and self-articulation of God to us in the incarnation of his Word and Truth in Jesus Christ. Hence theological concepts and statements may have reference to God only as they have a co-reference to this world of contingent objectivity and intelligibility, i.e., to the truth of created being. If they really are to refer to God, however, that reference must be primary, and this co-reference must be subordinated to it and allowed to serve it. That is, they must have an open or free reference to God, for knowledge of God and speech about him may not be dragged down and subordinated to the truths of created being. We may express this in another way, by saying that our knowledge of God is characterized by a mediated—not an unmediated—immediacy of God's self-revelation. God does not overwhelm us by an unmediated self-unveiling in his ultimate Truth, but reveals himself to us in such a way as not to disrupt the created structures of objectivity and intelligibility to which we belong as his creatures. He tempers or adapts knowledge of himself to us in such a way that he gives us immediate contact with him *through* the medium of the created order. While the contingent objectivities and intelligibilities of that order in themselves may have only an intramundane reference, they are nevertheless given an openness or freedom in reference beyond themselves through the creative power of God's self-revelation through them—but that is, then, an openness or freedom that is objectively controlled by his Truth. In this way the created truths assimilated to the manifestation and articulation of God's Truth, with which we are concerned in the interpretation of divine revelation through the Holy Scriptures, are invested with an authoritative reference to God grounded in his own ultimate Authority and Majesty. They fulfill that divinely given function, however, by subordinating themselves to and serving that ultimate Authority and not by arrogating it to themselves, for otherwise they would usurp and betray the Truth.

Let us consider the implication of this for theological concepts and statements. We recall that a statement is true when it signifies rightly, or as it ought, in accordance with what is the case, i.e., with the truth of created being, as Anselm used to express it. It signifies, however, in a double way: one way is through a relation of necessity under the determination of the nature of things, and one through a relation of freedom in which it fulfills an obligation demanded of it by a rightness or truth independent of it.[13] Now insofar as theological concepts and statements signify the truth of created being—that is, the objectivity and intelligibility of the created order in which God's ultimate Truth condescends to reveal himself to us—they fall under the constraint of that created truth and must be obedient to it, otherwise they would not signify rightly or truthfully. But insofar as that created truth refers beyond itself to the uncreated Truth of God, theological concepts and statements are summoned to assent to that transcendent reference in meeting their obligation toward it. Theological concepts and statements, however, would ultimately be empty and certainly false if their reference were cut short at the level of created truths, so that their objectivities and intelligibilities were treated as if they were not open to or free to serve transcendent Truth beyond themselves and were not subordinate to his Authority.

The truths of theological statement and formulation are what they ought to be when they serve the truths of being in God's objective self-revelation to us in this contingent world, and these truths of created being are what they ought to be when they serve the ultimate Truth of God himself. This hierarchic structure of levels of truth, as we have seen, means that truths of statement and all truths of created being serve the ultimate Truth, while the ultimate Truth cannot be brought under obligation to, or under the control of, the truths of created being or the truths of statement. But when this structure becomes inverted, then we attempt to subordinate the ultimate Truth to the truths of the creature and his statements, and we become entangled in a perverted authoritarianism in which we impose the preconceived patterns of our own devising or self-understanding upon God's self-revelation, and we clamp down our own independent formulations upon the substance of the faith.

It may help us here to draw a couple of distinctions: between primary and secondary authority, and between the authoritative and the authoritarian. According to biblical teaching, all authority *(exousia)* derives from God himself. He alone is primary or ultimate Authority, but there are secondary authorities or delegated authorities whose function it is to serve his supreme Authority, and they function authoritatively when they serve that divine Authority in such a way as not to obscure it but to let it appear in all God's ultimate Prerogative and Majesty and to be acknowledged as such. However, when these secondary authorities arrogate to themselves the authority delegated to them, thus constituting themselves authorities in their own right, then they become perverted "authorities of darkness," as the New Testament speaks of them. Thus instead of serving the ultimate Authority which brings freedom, they exercise an authoritarian tyranny which demands unreasoning submission.

It is in this light that the New Testament presents the unique Authority of Jesus Christ, which is characterized by an authoritativeness that astonished people around him and contrasted sharply with the authority of the Scribes and Pharisees, for theirs was merely authoritarian and enslaved the consciences of men and women. It is in a similar light that the authority of the law is presented by Paul. The law derives from God, and behind it stands all the divine Majesty and Holiness, which it is the function of the law to reveal and serve. But, owing to the dialectic of sin, the law tends to be treated as an authority in itself. When this happens, it can even become "the strength of sin" (I Cor. 15:56), for then it exercises such an authoritarian tyranny over people's conscience that it enslaves them and separates them from direct relation to God. Regarded in this autonomous status, as an independent authority on its own, the law becomes a "demonic" authority from which we are redeemed only through the blood of Christ. The important point for us to notice in this biblical teaching is that even the divinely promulgated law and the divinely appointed institutions, such as the Temple authorities, can become entangled in a situation where, instead of being genuinely authoritative, they have become authoritarian, and where, instead of serving the primary or ultimate Authority of God and the freedom to which he creatively gives rise, they have usurped his Prerogative and come to play an oppressive role.[14]

It is essentially the same basic issue at stake in our handling of the relations between the truth of statement and the truth of being, and between the truth of created being and the Truth of God's Being—whether we are concerned with the interpretation of God's self-revelation in the Bible or formulating our understanding of the truths thereby conveyed to us. Theological formulation takes place not simply on the dictates of biblical statements but through a movement of interpretative and elucidatory penetration into the inner intelligibility of divine revelation, in which we allow our own thinking and articulation to be molded pliantly and obediently by the incarnate Truth of God in Jesus Christ and thus to take their basic form from the inner Word or Speech in the very Being of God. In this movement of understanding the self-revelation of God we do not operate with a criterion of truth lodged in the subjects of the interpreters or theologians (whether as individuals or as the church)— for we are thrown back objectively upon the Truth and Word of God himself, who forces us to call in question all our preconceptions and prejudgments as he declares himself to us in the present. In theological formulation we do not operate with definitions of the truth that are regarded as its necessary extensions, but with statements that serve the Truth in its own inexhaustible Reality and Intelligibility, in such a way that they become progressively refined media through which God imprints his Truth more deeply upon our minds in the power of his own self-interpretation and self-explication. Since the ultimate truth of theological formulations does not reside in these formulations as such but in him whom they serve, they are truthfully related to the Truth only when they make clear that they are relativized by the Truth. The fact that they fall short of the Truth is an essential element in their propriety and precision, for therein they point to their justification in God alone. It is this which confers upon them their openness and freedom to serve him.

Notes

1. The Bounds of Christian Theology

1. John Duns Scotus, *Ordinatio,* prol.n.141, 168; *De primo principio,* c.4, n.36. See further, T. F. Torrance, "Intuitive and Abstractive Knowledge from Duns Scotus to John Calvin," in C. Balić (ed.), *De doctrina Ioannis Duns Scoti,* Vol. IV (Rome, 1968), pp. 299f.

2. John Duns Scotus, *Reportata,* prol.q.2, n.17.

3. See further, T. F. Torrance, *Conflict and Agreement in the Church,* Vol. 2 (London: Lutterworth Press, 1960), pp. 82–92.

4. Cf. here the Athanasian doctrine of God, in T. F. Torrance, *Theology in Reconciliation: Essays Towards Evangelical and Catholic Unity in East and West* (Wm. B. Eerdmans Publishing Co., 1976), pp. 220ff.; and further my "Toward an Ecumenical Consensus on the Trinity," *Theologische Zeitschrift* (Basel), Vol. 31 (1975), pp. 337–350; and *The Ground and Grammar of Theology* (Charlottesville, Va.: University Press of Virginia, 1980), Ch. 6, pp. 146ff.

5. This point is well made by Karl Rahner, *The Trinity* (London: Burns & Oates, 1970; Seabury Press, 1970), pp. 36ff.

6. See again Torrance, *The Ground and Grammar of Theology,* Ch. 1, "Man, the Priest of Creation," pp. 1ff.

7. Cf. Richard P. Feynman, *The Character of Physical Law* (London: British Broadcasting Corp., 1965; Cambridge, Mass.: MIT Press, 1967), "The Relation of Mathematics to Physics," pp. 35ff.; and my own discussion of "Word and Number," *Christian Theology and Scientific Culture* (Belfast, 1980; New York, 1981), pp. 105ff.

8. On the formal use of symbols and the problems that such a

split gives rise to, see E. H. Hutten, *The Origins of Science: An Inquiry Into the Foundations of Western Thought* (London: George Allen & Unwin, 1962; New York: Humanities Press, 1963), pp. 115ff. and 164ff.

9. See T. F. Torrance, *Divine and Contingent Order* (1981), passim; also *The Ground and Grammar of Theology,* Chs. 2–5; and *Christian Theology and Scientific Culture,* Chs. 1–2.

10. For the implications of Michael Polanyi's thought along these lines, see the various contributions to T. F. Torrance (ed.), *Belief in Science and in Christian Life: The Relevance of Michael Polanyi's Thought for Christian Faith and Life* (Edinburgh: Handsel Press; New York: Columbia University Press, 1980); and my essay, "The Place of Michael Polanyi in the Modern Philosophy of Science," *Ethics in Science and Medicine,* Vol. 7 (1980), pp. 57–95.

11. Cf. Albert Einstein, *Ideas and Opinions* (1954; London: Souvenir Press, 1973), on "Geometry and Experience," pp. 232ff.

12. Einstein, *Ideas and Opinions,* "Physics and Reality," pp. 290–323; Michael Polanyi, *The Study of Man* (London: Routledge & Kegan Paul; Chicago: University of Chicago Press, 1959), pp. 46ff., 93ff.; *The Tacit Dimension* (New York: Doubleday & Co., 1966; London: Routledge & Kegan Paul, 1967), pp. 32ff.; and *Knowing and Being: Essays,* ed. by Marjorie Grene (London: Routledge & Kegan Paul; Chicago: University of Chicago Press, 1969), pp. 153ff., 216ff., 225ff., etc.

13. I have discussed this in *The Ground and Grammar of Theology,* Ch. 6, pp. 146ff.

14. See the valuable discussions of this in various works by F. S. C. Northrop, for example, in *The Logic of the Sciences and the Humanities* (Macmillan Co., 1947); *Man, Nature and God: A Quest for Life's Meaning* (Simon & Schuster, 1962), and his contribution to the volume edited by P. A. Schilpp, *Albert Einstein: Philosopher-Scientist,* 2d ed. (Cambridge University Press; New York: Tudor Publishing Co., 1952), pp. 387–408.

15. Northrop, *Man, Nature and God,* pp. 34ff.

16. Polanyi, *Knowing and Being,* pp. 144ff., 198f., 203, 207.

17. Boethius, *De personis et duabus naturis* II, PL 64, 1343C.

18. Richard of St.-Victor, *De Trinitate* IV.22, 24. Cf. also John Duns Scotus, *Ordinatio* 1.23, q.1.

19. See Torrance (ed.), *Belief in Science and in Christian Life,* pp. 141f. For the way in which Polanyi's "personal model" of thought

complements that of Einstein in this respect, see my *Christian Theology and Scientific Culture,* pp. 61ff.

2. Theological Questions to Biblical Scholars

1. For a fuller discussion of this, see Torrance (ed.), *Belief in Science and in Christian Life: The Relevance of Michael Polanyi's Thought for Christian Faith and Life,* pp. 7ff.; and also my discussion of "Ultimate Beliefs and the Scientific Revolution," *Cross Currents* (New York), Vol. 30 (1980), No. 1.

2. Michael Polanyi, *Personal Knowledge* (London: Routledge & Kegan Paul; Chicago: University of Chicago Press, 1958), pp. 95ff., 187ff., 155ff., 264ff., 286ff., etc. See also Polanyi, *The Tacit Dimension,* passim.

3. For the following see my essay, "Theological Realism," in S. Sutherland and B. Hebblethwaite (eds.), *The Philosophical Frontiers of Christian Theology* (Cambridge University Press, 1981), pp. 169–196.

4. For discussions of this see Karl Barth, *Church Dogmatics,* I/1, 2d ed. (new tr. by Geoffrey W. Bromiley; Edinburgh: T. & T. Clark, 1975), pp. 402ff.; and Dietrich Bonhoeffer, *Christology* (London: William Collins Sons & Co., 1966; also published under the title *Christ the Center;* Harper & Row, 1966), pp. 78ff., 85ff.

5. Serious problems did arise in the fifth century, in the West with Augustinian dualism, and in the East with the resurgence of Neoplatonic dualism within Byzantine thought. So far as conciliar theology is concerned, this problem is already evident in the Council of Chalcedon, or at least in the famous "Tome of Leo" in terms of which Chalcedonian thought was given a dualist interpretation, which in the East led to the split between the more dualist Byzantines and the more realist "non-Chalcedonians" who based their thought on Cyril of Alexandria, e.g., Severus of Antioch.

6. See the illuminating note by Hans-Georg Gadamer, *Wahrheit und Methode* (Tübingen, 1960), pp. 474ff.

7. Cf. Polanyi, *Personal Knowledge,* pp. 57, 91; *Knowing and Being,* pp. 193, 207.

8. The analogy is taken from John Calvin, *Institute* I.6.1; 14.1; and *Commentary on Genesis,* introductory "Argument."

9. Plato, *Cratylus,* 383–392, 430–432, 438–440.

10. For the importance of this feedback from things to words in our understanding of them, cf. the remark of Whitehead: "Thus

in the use of language there is a double symbolic reference—from things to words on the part of the speaker, and from words back to things on the part of the listener" (Alfred North Whitehead, *Symbolism: Its Meaning and Effect,* Cambridge, 1927, p. 14).

11. Cf. Henry Margenau: "To achieve *objectivity* of basic description, the theory must confer *relativity* upon the domain of immediate observations" (Schilpp, ed., *Albert Einstein: Philosopher-Scientist,* 2d ed., p. 254).

12. Einstein, *Ideas and Opinions,* "On the Method of Theoretical Physics," p. 275.

13. This point was made long ago with incisive force by Hilary of Poitiers, in *De Trinitate* II.1–5. He does not hesitate, however, to point out the danger this involves.

14. Cf. Walter R. Thorson, "The Concept of Truth in the Natural Sciences," *Themelios* (Lausanne), Vol. 5 (1968), No. 2, p. 35.

15. Alfred North Whitehead, *Process and Reality* (Cambridge, 1930), especially Part I, Ch. 2; Part II, Chs. 1, 7, 9. Whitehead's complaint is that we are apt to be imprisoned in the structure of a language characterized by static connections which fail to cope with the dynamic relations of empirical events. He also argues that these features lead us into the fallacy of the bifurcation of nature; see *The Concept of Nature* (Cambridge, 1920), Chs. 1 and 2. See especially the extensive discussion of these questions by Alfred Korzybski, *Science and Sanity: An Introduction to Non-Aristotelian Systems and General Semantics* (Lakeville, Conn.: Institute of General Semantics, 4th ed. 1958).

16. Cf. Alfred North Whitehead, *The Principle of Relativity* (Cambridge, 1922), pp. 13f. See also Northrop, *Man, Nature and God,* pp. 74ff.

17. See Otto Neugebauer, *The Exact Sciences in Antiquity,* 2d ed. (Providence, R. I.: Brown University Press, 1957), in which he shows the cultural connection between algebra and Babylonian language, and contrasts this with the relation of linear mathematics to Greek language. It is significant that Richard Feynman, in *The Character of Physical Law,* points out that in modern physics we need the Babylonian mathematical method rather than the Greek (pp. 46f.).

18. James Barr, *The Semantics of Biblical Language* (Oxford University Press, 1961). Barr's ill-judged attack on the lessons to be learned from etymology contrasts with Plato's wise judgment that we are often put on the right track of the objective semantic

reference of a term by examining archaic forms (*Cratylus* 401C).

19. Kurt Gödel, *On Formally Undecidable Propositions of Principia Mathematica and Related Systems*, tr. by Bernard Meltzer (Edinburgh: Oliver & Boyd, 1962; New York: Basic Books, 1963). See also Ernest Nagel and James R. Newman, *Gödel's Proof* (New York University Press, 1958; London: Routledge & Kegan Paul, 1959), and my discussion in the paper, "The Place of Michael Polanyi in the Modern Philosophy of Science," *Ethics in Science and Medicine* (Oxford), Vol. 7 (1980), pp. 75ff.

20. Plato, *Phaedrus* 274–276. Plato describes the writer who does not rise above his writings as a mere *logographos*.

21. Alfred North Whitehead, *Modes of Thought* (Cambridge, 1938), p. 51.

22. See the enlightening Terry Lectures by Walter J. Ong, *The Presence of the Word* (Yale University Press, 1967), p. 74.

23. Cf. Milič Čapek, *The Philosophical Impact of Contemporary Physics* (D. Van Nostrand Co., 1961), pp. 170f. See Ong, op. cit., p. 128.

24. Cf. Fritjof Capra, *The Tao of Physics: An Exploration of the Parallels Between Modern Physics and Eastern Mysticism* (London: Wildwood House, 1975; Berkeley, Calif.: Shambhala Publications, 1976).

25. Hilary of Poitiers, *De Trinitate* X.51.

26. T. F. Torrance, *Theological Science* (Oxford University Press, 1969), pp. 23f., 40, 159, 161, 177, 182f., 192, 233.

27. John Calvin, *Institute* I.7.5, which appears to be indebted to Athanasius, *De incarnatione* 3.

28. Anselm of Canterbury, *Monologion* 10; *De grammatico* 7. See further my essay "The Place of Word and Truth in Theological Inquiry According to St. Anselm," in *Studia mediaevalia et mariologica P. Carolo Balić OFM septuagesimum explenti annum dicata* (Rome, 1971), pp. 141ff., 147ff.

29. See my essay on Major's thought, "La Philosophie et la Theologie de Jean Mair ou Major (1469–1550)," *Archives de Philosophie* (Paris), Oct.–Dec., 1969 (Vol. 32), pp. 531–547, and Avril–Juin 1970 (Vol. 33), pp. 261–293.

30. *The Collected Works of St. John of the Cross*, tr. by Kieran Kavanaugh and Otilio Rodriguez (London, 1964; New York: Doubleday & Co., 1964), pp. 110ff., 129ff., 137, 152, 215f., 224f., 471f., 515, 526, 544f., 610f., 630.

31. See above all Karl Barth, *Church Dogmatics*, I/2, Ch. III on

"Holy Scripture," and Ch. IV on "The Proclamation of the Church."

32. This is a distinction that derives from Wilhelm Herrmann, *Die Religion im Verhältnis zum Welterkennen und zur Sittlichkeit* (1879), p. 313; *The Communion of the Christian with God* (1886; tr. of 4th German ed., 1906), p. 114. Cf. also Martin Kähler, *The So-called Historical Jesus and the Historic, Biblical Christ,* tr. by Carl E. Braaten (1892; Fortress Press, 1964).

33. I have discussed this elsewhere in several places, but cf. my *Space, Time and Incarnation* (Oxford University Press, 1969); and *Space, Time and Resurrection* (Edinburgh: Handsel Press, 1976; Grand Rapids: Wm. B. Eerdmans Publishing Co., 1977).

34. See my *Space, Time and Incarnation,* Ch. 2; and "The Integration of Form in Natural and in Theological Science," *Science, Medicine and Man* (now *Ethics in Science and Medicine*) (Oxford), Vol. 1 (1973), pp. 143–172.

35. For the views of Rudolf Bultmann, see, e.g., his notorious essay "New Testament and Mythology," in *Kerygma and Myth: A Theological Debate,* ed. by H. W. Bartsch and tr. by R. H. Fuller (London: S.P.C.K., 1953; New York: Macmillan Co., 1954), pp. 1–44; or his *Jesus Christ and Mythology* (New York: Charles Scribner's Sons, 1958; London: SCM Press, 1960).

36. F. A. Hayek, *Law, Legislation and Liberty,* Vol. 1, *Rules and Order* (London: Routledge & Kegan Paul, 1973), p. 14.

37. Michael Dummett, "Biblical Exegesis and the Resurrection," *New Blackfriars* (London), Feb. 1977, p. 57.

38. Cf. my contribution to the forthcoming *Bo Reicke Festschrift* (Leiden: E. J. Brill), "The Historical Jesus from the Perspective of a Theologian."

3. A Realist Interpretation of God's Self-Revelation

1. For the following, see T. F. Torrance, *God and Rationality* (Oxford University Press, 1971), Ch. 6, pp. 137ff.

2. Cf. Georges Florovsky on "Revelation and Interpretation," Ch. 2 in his *Collected Works,* Vol. 1, *Bible, Church, Tradition: An Eastern Orthodox View* (Belmont, Mass.: Nordland Publishing Co., 1972), p. 21.

3. A full account of the actualization of God's self-revelation in Jesus Christ (which we cannot enter into here) must reckon with the fact that this is achieved within our estranged and impaired

existence, and, therefore, only through atoning reconciliation and sanctifying re-creation. This is why it would not be theologically proper to offer an account of the inspiration of the Holy Scriptures apart from a doctrine of atoning mediation between the Word of God and the word of man.

4. Cf. Bryan J. Gray, "Towards Better Ways of Reading the Bible," *Scottish Journal of Theology,* Vol. 33, No. 4 (1980), pp. 306f.

5. See Torrance, *Christian Theology and Scientific Culture,* Ch. 4 "Word and Number," pp. 105ff.

6. Torrance, *God and Rationality,* p. 152. See also T. F. Torrance, *Christ's Words* (Jedburgh, 1981).

7. Cf. Barth's discussion, *Church Dogmatics,* I/2 (1956), Ch. III on "Holy Scripture," pp. 457–537.

8. Michael Polanyi speaks of this as "sense-deprivation." See his *Knowing and Being,* pp. 185, 192.

9. Cf. again Michael Dummett, "Biblical Exegesis and the Resurrection," *New Blackfriars,* Feb. 1977, pp. 56ff.

10. See Paul Ricoeur, *Interpretation Theory: Discourse and the Surplus of Meaning* (Forth Worth, Tex.: Texas Christian University Press, 1976), pp. 87f.; and Gray, "Towards Better Ways of Reading the Bible," p. 305 (see note 4, above).

11. On this sense of commitment, see above all Polanyi, *Personal Knowledge,* especially Ch. 10, pp. 299ff.

12. I have in mind here the distinction drawn by I. A. Richards between "the *scientific* use of language" and "the *emotive* use of language" (*Principles of Literary Criticism,* 2d ed., repr. London: Routledge & Kegan Paul, 1960, p. 267).

13. For the following see my discussion on "The Hermeneutics of St. Athanasius," *Ekklesiastikos Pharos* (Addis Ababa), 1970, No. 1, pp. 446–468; No. 2–3, pp. 89–106; No. 4, pp. 237–249; 1971, No. 1, pp. 133–149.

14. Karl Barth, *The Word of God and the Word of Man* (London, 1928), Ch. II.

15. For full references to the following see my essay "The Implications of Oikonomia for Knowledge and Speech of God in Early Christian Theology," in Felix Christ (ed.), *Oikonomia. Heilsgeschichte als Thema der Theologie* (Hamburg-Bergstedt, 1967), pp. 223ff.

16. Cf. Aristotle, *Topica* I.100A–B, which Clement has in mind. This is combined in the patristic tradition with the use of Isa. 7.9

(LXX): "If you do not believe, neither will you understand." See further, Torrance, *Belief in Science and in Christian Life*, pp. 3f.; and E. F. Osborn, *The Philosophy of Clement of Alexandria* (Cambridge University Press, 1957), pp. 131ff.

17. Clement's term for this is *prolepsis*, which is not to be understood as a "preconception" but as a forward leap of the mind under the pressure of reality itself (Osborn, op. cit., p. 224). The same point is finally made by Augustine, in rejection of the Platonic notion, in *Retractationes* 14.4. See R. A. Markus in A. H. Armstrong (ed.), *The Cambridge History of Later Greek and Early Medieval Philosophy* (Cambridge University Press, 1967), p. 366.

18. Cf. Polanyi, *Knowing and Being*, p. 189: "An unintelligible text referring to an unintelligible matter presents us with a dual problem. Both halves of such a problem jointly guide our minds towards solving them and will in fact be solved jointly by the understanding of the objects referred to and the words referring to it. The meaning of the things and of the terms designating them is discovered at the same time."

19. Cf. Ricoeur, *Interpretation Theory*, pp. 22f., on the psychologizing conception of hermeneutics.

20. The argument here, of course, is circular, but it is properly so. The form of the argument is similar to that in any coherent system operating with ultimate axioms or beliefs which cannot be derived or justified from any other ground than that which they themselves constitute. See my *Space, Time and Resurrection*, pp. 14f. It is this point—that we must operate within the scope of a coherent outlook or system—which explains why this discussion started with an account of the correlation between the Bible and God's self-revelation, for it is only as we take that seriously that we may operate inside the circle of biblical thought as it interprets and presents itself to us.

21. Torrance, "The Hermeneutics of St. Athanasius." For references to this essay, see *Ekklesiastikos Pharos*, 1970, No. 2–3, pp. 95ff., 104ff. (See note 13, above.)

22. Cf. here Hilary of Poitiers, *De Trinitate* 1.30; 4.27f.; 5.18f., 24f., etc. And see my "Hermeneutics, or the Interpretation of Biblical and Theological Statements According to Hilary of Poitiers," *Abba Salama* (Athens), Vol. 6 (1975), pp. 40f. For the patristic concept of economy and its development, see G. L. Prestige, *God in Patristic Thought*, 2d ed. (London: S.P.C.K., 1952), pp. 57ff., 62f., 98ff.

23. See Athanasius, *Contra Arianos* 11.6, 9, 45, 51, 53, 75, 76. In these passages the term "economy" has a strong soteriological slant, for it expresses the form which God's activity has taken for our sake. It is in that "economic" sense that we are to understand the coming of Christ in the form of a "servant," for example; far from being merely an appearance or a temporary expedient, the incarnate humiliation of the Son was the saving reality of God's presence among us. That is what controls the epistemological sense of Athanasius' use of the term.

24. Cf. Athanasius, *De sententia Dionysii,* where "economic" is contrasted with "putative" or what is merely "conceptual" (1.23f.).

25. Athanasius, *Ad Epictetum* 2, 7. See also the document *Contra Apollinarem* I.10, 12, 17; II.5. This corresponds to the contrast between "putative" and "real" referred to in note 24. For the Athanasian use of technical terms in theology, see my *Theology in Reconciliation,* pp. 239ff.

26. See Athanasius' essay on this logion, *In illud omnia.*

27. For the process of thought at work here, see Torrance, *The Ground and Grammar of Theology,* pp. 156ff., where I show that it is strikingly similar to that described by Einstein in discussing the process of scientific thought, in his essay "Physics and Reality" (*Ideas and Opinions,* pp. 290ff.).

28. Torrance, *Theological Science,* pp. 164ff., 226ff., 246ff.

29. Gödel, *On Formally Undecidable Propositions of Principia Mathematica and Related Systems.* See also my *Theological Science,* pp. 255ff.; and "The Place of Michael Polanyi in the Modern Philosophy of Science," *Ethics in Science and Medicine,* Vol. 7 (1980), pp. 74–81.

30. John Duns Scotus, *Ordinatio* I d.2 n.1 5–17; d.3 n.230–234.

31. See Clement of Alexandria, *Stromateis* VII.16. Strictly speaking, the truth interprets itself to us (I.7). The last two books of Clement's *Stromateis,* and Athanasius' twin works *Contra gentes* and *De incarnatione,* are clear examples of how Christian thought operates, not by deriving knowledge abstractively or deductively from Holy Scripture, but under the guidance of the Scriptures and within the field of faith in God through Christ by penetrating into the intrinsic intelligibility of the Truth itself, so that it may shine to us in its own light and power. Cf. here my *Theology in Reconciliation,* pp. 255ff.

32. Cf. especially the first two books of Hilary of Poitiers, *De Trinitate.*

33. Cf. Hippolytus, *Adversus haereses* X.5.2; Eusebius, *Historia ecclesiae* 4.23.4, etc.

34. See Oscar Cullmann, *The Earliest Christian Confessions,* tr. by J. K. S. Reid (London: Lutterworth Press, 1948); and J. N. D. Kelly, *Early Christian Creeds* (London: Longmans, Green & Co., 1950).

4. Truth and Justification in Doctrinal Formulation

1. *Ioannis Calvini Opera Selecta,* Vol. 1, ed. by P. Barth (1926), pp. 21–36.

2. *Analogia fidei* is thus also the equivalent of *obedientia fidei* (ibid., p. 27).

3. Cf. Anselm, "How then has anything true at all been found concerning the supreme Being, if what has been found is so far removed from him?" *Monologion* 65 (*Opera Omnia*, ed. by F. S. Schmitt, 1938; repr. 1946; Vol. I, p. 76). See also my *Theological Science,* pp. 145f.

4. Anselm, *De Veritate, Opera Omnia,* Vol. I, pp. 173–199. For the following see my essays "The Ethical Implications of Anselm's De Veritate" (*Theologische Zeitschrift,* Vol. 24, 1968, pp. 309–319) and "The Place of Word and Truth in Theological Inquiry According to St. Anselm" (in *Studia Mediaevalia et Mariologica* [Rome], 1971, pp. 134–160).

5. Anselm, *Cur Deus homo?,* commendatio operis, *Opera Omnia,* Vol. I, p. 40.

6. Anselm, *Monologion* 10, *Opera Omnia,* Vol. I, p. 25. For further references see my essay "The Place of Word and Truth in Theological Inquiry According to St. Anselm," pp. 136ff. (See note 4, above.)

7. For Anselm's stress on experience and prayer see the *Epistola de incarnatione Verbi* (*Opera Omnia,* Vol. II, pp. 1ff.). This is an aspect of Anselm's thought stressed by Karl Barth in *Anselm: Fides Quaerens Intellectum,* tr. by Ian Robertson (London: SCM Press, 1960), pp. 35f.

8. Barth, *Church Dogmatics,* I/1, 2d ed. (1975), pp. 138f.

9. Cf. here Polanyi, *The Study of Man,* pp. 96f.

10. This is the epistemological implication of the "I, yet not I, but Christ" of Paul's epistle to the Galatians (Gal. 2:20).

11. See Calvin's discussion of theological language used to speak of the Trinity (*Institute* I.13.5, 18, etc.). Cf. my *Theology in Reconstruction* (London: SCM Press, 1965; Grand Rapids, Mich.: Wm. B. Eerdmans Publishing Co., 1966), "Knowledge of God and Speech About Him According to John Calvin," pp. 83f.

12. See especially Michael Polanyi, *Science, Faith and Society* (with a new introduction by the author; University of Chicago Press, 1964), Ch. II, "Authority and Conscience," and Ch. III, "Dedication or Servitude." And see further, Torrance (ed.), *Belief in Science and in Christian Life: The Relevance of Michael Polanyi's Thought for Christian Faith and Life,* pp. 11ff., 146f.

13. We are familiar with this double relation of necessity and freedom in our ordinary acts of perception. We cannot but see things around us (table, chairs, books, etc.) as they force themselves on our vision. However, this does not mean that we are not free. In addition to being compelled to see them, we are obliged to think of them and act toward them in accordance with their natures, that is, rightly and objectively and indeed rationally. Thus we freely meet an obligation as well as suffer a compulsion. Without the latter we could not do the former. Freedom and objective order go together.

14. See my discussion of "Truth and Authority," *Irish Theological Quarterly,* Vol. 39, No. 3 (1972), pp. 239ff.

Index of Names

Index of Subjects